DEFINING MOMENTS
WOMEN'S SUFFRAGE

DEFINING MOMENTS
WOMEN'S SUFFRAGE

Jeff Hill

615 Griswold, Detroit MI 48226

Omnigraphics, Inc.

Kevin Hillstrom, *Series Editor*
Cherie D. Abbey, *Managing Editor*

Peter E. Ruffner, *Publisher*
Frederick G. Ruffner, Jr., *Chairman*
Matthew P. Barbour, *Senior Vice President*

Kay Gill, *Vice President – Directories*
Elizabeth Barbour, *Research and Permissions
    Coordinator*
David P. Bianco, *Marketing Director*
Leif Gruenberg, *Development Manager*
Kevin Hayes, *Operations Manager*

Barry Puckett, *Librarian*
Cherry Stockdale, *Permissions Assistant*
Shirley Amore, Don Brown, John L. Chetcuti, Kevin
    Glover, Martha Johns, Kirk Kauffman, *Adminis-
    trative Staff*

Hill, Jeff, 1962-
    Women's suffrage / Jeff Hill.
        p. cm. -- (Defining moments)
    Summary: "Examines the history of the women's suffrage movement and its impact on American
life and society. Features include narrative overview, biographical profiles, primary source documents, detailed chronology, and annotated sources for further study"--Provided by publisher.
    Includes bibliographical references and index.
    ISBN 0-7808-0776-6 (hardcover : alk. paper)
    1. Women--Suffrage--United States--History. 2. Suffragists--United States--Biography. I. Title. II.
Series.
    JK1896.H54 2006
    324.6'23'0973--dc22
                                                                                        2005024812

TABLE OF CONTENTS

PRIMARY SOURCES

PREFACE

Throughout the course of America's existence, its people, culture, and institutions have been periodically challenged—and in many cases transformed—by profound historical events. Some of these momentous events, such as women's suffrage, the civil rights movement, and U.S. involvement in World War II, have invigorated the nation and strengthened American confidence and capabilities. Others, such as the McCarthy era, the Vietnam War, and Watergate, have prompted troubled assessments and heated debates about the country's core beliefs and character.

Some of these defining moments in American history were years or even decades in the making. The Harlem Renaissance and the New Deal, for example, unfurled over the span of several years, while the American labor movement and the Cold War evolved over the course of decades. Other defining moments, such as the Cuban missile crisis and the terrorist attacks of September 11, 2001, transpired over a matter of days or weeks.

But although significant differences exist among these events in terms of their duration and their place in the timeline of American history, all share the same basic characteristic: they transformed the United States' political, cultural, and social landscape for future generations of Americans.

Taking heed of this fundamental reality, American citizens, schools, and other institutions are increasingly emphasizing the importance of understanding our nation's history. Omnigraphics' *Defining Moments* series was created for the express purpose of meeting this growing appetite for authoritative, useful historical resources. This series, which focuses on the most pivotal events in U.S. history from the 20th century forward, will be of enduring value to anyone interested in learning more about America's past—and in understanding how those historical events continue to reverberate in the 21st century.

Each individual volume of *Defining Moments* provides a valuable resource for readers interested in learning more about the most profound events in our nation's history. Each volume is organized into three distinct sections—Narrative Overview, Biographies, and Primary Sources.

- The **Narrative Overview** provides readers with a detailed, factual account of the origins and progression of the "defining moment" being examined. It also explores the event's lasting impact on America's political and cultural landscape.

- The **Biographies** section provides valuable biographical background on leading figures associated with the event in question. Each biography concludes with a list of sources for further information on the profiled individual.

- The **Primary Sources** section collects a wide variety of pertinent primary source materials from the era under discussion, including official documents, papers and resolutions, letters, oral histories, memoirs, editorials, and other important works.

Individually, each of these sections is a rich resource for users. Together, they provide an authoritative, balanced, and absorbing examination of some of the most significant events in U.S. history.

Other notable features contained within each volume in the series include a glossary of important individuals, places, and terms; a detailed chronology featuring page references to relevant sections of the narrative; an annotated bibliography of sources for further study; an extensive general bibliography that reflects the wide range of historical sources consulted by the author; and a subject index.

Acknowledgements

This series was developed in consultation with a distinguished Advisory Board comprised of public librarians, school librarians, and educators. They evaluated the series as it developed, and their comments and suggestions were invaluable throughout the production process. Any errors in this and other volumes in the series are ours alone. Following is a list of board members who contributed to the *Defining Moments* series:

Gail Beaver, M.A., M.A.L.S.
Adjunct Lecturer, University of Michigan
Ann Arbor, MI

Melissa C. Bergin, L.M.S., NBCT
Niskayuna High School
Niskayuna, NY

Rose Davenport, M.S.L.S., Ed. Specialist
Library Media Specialist
Pershing High School Library
Detroit, MI

Karen Imarisio, A.M.L.S.
Assistant Head of Adult Services
Bloomfield Twp. Public Library
Bloomfield Hills, MI

Nancy Larsen, M.L.S., M.S. Ed.
Library Media Specialist
Clarkston High School
Clarkston, MI

Marilyn Mast, M.I.L.S.
Kingswood Campus Librarian
Cranbrook Kingswood Upper School
Bloomfield Hills, MI

Rosemary Orlando, M.L.I.S.
Assistant Director
St. Clair Shores Public Library
St. Clair Shores, MI

Comments and Suggestions

We welcome your comments on *Defining Moments: Women's Suffrage* and suggestions for other events in U.S. history that warrant treatment in the *Defining Moments* series. Correspondence should be addressed to:

Editor, *Defining Moments*
Omnigraphics, Inc.
615 Griswold
Detroit, MI 48226
E-mail: editorial@omnigraphics.com

HOW TO USE THIS BOOK

*D*efining Moments: Women's Suffrage provides users with a detailed and authoritative overview of the women's suffrage movement, as well as the principal figures involved in this pivotal era in U.S. history. The preparation and arrangement of this volume—and all other books in the *Defining Moments* series—reflect an emphasis on providing a thorough and objective account of events that shaped our nation, presented in an easy-to-use reference work.

Defining Moments: Women's Suffrage is divided into three primary sections. The first of these sections, the **Narrative Overview**, provides a detailed, factual account of the history of women's legal and political rights in America and the milestone events on the path to women's suffrage. It explains the mid-nineteenth century alliance between suffragettes and abolitionists, explores how the different beliefs of suffrage leaders led to deep schisms in the movement, discusses the various strategies employed by pro- and anti-suffrage organizations to advance their respective causes, and examines the enduring impact of women's suffrage on American culture and politics.

The second section, **Biographies**, provides valuable biographical background on leading figures involved in the movement. Individuals profiled include suffrage pioneers Susan B. Anthony and Elizabeth Cady Stanton, activist and presidential candidate Victoria C. Woodhull, and militant organizer Alice Paul. Each biography concludes with a list of sources for further information on the profiled individual.

The third section, **Primary Sources**, collects essential and enlightening documents that provide perspective on the century-long drive to secure women's voting rights. Featured sources include the Declaration of Sentiments from the historic 1848 Women's Rights Convention held in Seneca Falls, New York; Elizabeth Cady Stanton's 1869 address to the National

Woman Suffrage Convention; Susan B. Anthony's reaction to her 1872 conviction for unlawful voting; and suffrage activist Ernestine Hara Kettler's recollection of her 1917 imprisonment for picketing the White House. Other primary sources featured in *Defining Moments: Women's Suffrage* include excerpts from official documents, papers, memoirs, speeches, and other important works.

Other valuable features in *Defining Moments: Women's Suffrage* include the following:

- Attribution and referencing of primary sources and other quoted material to help guide users to other valuable historical research resources.

- Glossary of Important People, Places, and Terms.

- Detailed Chronology of events with a *see reference* feature. Under this arrangement, events listed in the chronology include a reference to page numbers within the Narrative Overview wherein users can find additional information on the event in question.

- Photographs of the leading figures and major events of the era.

- Sources for Further Study, an annotated list of noteworthy works.

- Extensive bibliography of works consulted in the creation of this book, including books, periodicals, Internet sites, and videotape materials.

- A Subject Index.

Editor's Note: This volume includes quoted material containing racial epithets and offensive language. We regret any pain created by the inclusion of this language. We felt, however, that it was important to include this material because it reflects representative views and prejudices of the era.

IMPORTANT PEOPLE, PLACES, AND TERMS

Adams, Abigail
Wife of American patriot and U.S. president John Adams who advocated better treatment for women

Addams, Jane
Social activist and suffragist who served as a leader in the National American Woman Suffrage Association in the early 1900s

American Equal Rights Association
Organization formed in the mid-1860s to promote the rights of both women and African Americans

American Woman Suffrage Association (AWSA)
Organization founded by Lucy Stone and other women's rights activists in 1869

Anthony, Susan B.
Women's suffrage pioneer who headed the National Woman's Suffrage Association (NWSA) and the National American Woman Suffrage Association (NAWSA)

Beecher, Henry Ward
Popular minister who served as president of the American Woman Suffrage Association in the early 1870s

Blackstone, Sir William
Eighteenth-century British legal scholar whose views on the legal status of women were influential in North America

Blackwell, Alice Stone
Suffragist and daughter of Lucy Stone and Henry Blackwell

Blackwell, Henry
Abolitionist, women's rights activist, and husband of Lucy Stone

Blatch, Harriot Stanton
Suffragist and daughter of Elizabeth Cady Stanton

Butler, Benjamin
United States Senator and friend of Victoria Woodhull

Brown, Antoinette
Christian minister and women's rights activist in the mid-1800s (also known as Antoinette Brown Blackwell)

Burns, Lucy
Leader of the Congressional Union and the National Woman's Party in the 1910s

Catt, Carrie Chapman
Two-time president of the National American Woman Suffrage Association (NAWSA) in the early 1900s

Clay, Laura
Kentucky suffragist who promoted suffrage on the state level but opposed the Nineteenth Amendment

Congressional Union
Suffrage organization founded by Alice Paul in 1913

Davis, Paulina Wright
Woman's rights activist in the mid-nineteenth century

Dickinson, Anna E.
Famous public speaker of the 1860s and 1870s who advocated abolition and women's rights

Douglass, Frederick
African American abolitionist and women's rights activist in the mid-1800s

Equality League of Self-Supporting Women
Organization founded in 1907 by Harriot Stanton Blatch that emphasized reaching working-class women in suffrage efforts

Fifteenth Amendment
Constitutional amendment ratified in 1870 that states that a citizen's right to vote cannot be denied on account of "race, color, or previous condition of servitude"

Fourteenth Amendment
Constitutional amendment that strengthened African American voting rights; ratified in 1868

Gage, Frances D.
Women's suffrage activist based in Ohio in the mid-1800s

Garrison, William Lloyd
Antislavery pioneer who was also active in the women's right movement in the mid-1800s

Greeley, Horace
Publisher of the *New York Tribune*

Grimké, Sarah and Angelina
Sisters who were active in the antislavery movement in the 1830s and also criticized the inferior status of women

Kelly, Abby
Groundbreaking female abolitionist active in the mid-1800s (also known as Abby Kelly Foster)

Milholland, Inez
Member of the National Woman's Party who died while campaigning for suffrage in 1916

Minor vs. Happersett
1875 Supreme Court case that determined that the Fourteenth and Fifteenth Amendments do not give women the right to vote

Mott, Lucretia
Quaker abolitionist and women's rights activist in the mid-1800s

National American Woman Suffrage Association (NAWSA)
Unified organization formed in 1890 by the merger of the National Woman's Suffrage Association (NWSA) and the American Woman Suffrage Association (AWSA)

National Association of Colored Women
Umbrella group for African American women's clubs that advocated suffrage; founded in 1896

National Association Opposed to Woman Suffrage
Anti-suffragist lobbying group founded in 1911

National Woman's Suffrage Association (NWSA)
Organization founded by Elizabeth Cady Stanton and Susan B. Anthony in 1869

National Woman's Party
Suffrage Organization led by Alice Paul that evolved from the Congressional Union in 1916

National Women's Christian Temperance Union
Anti-alcohol organization founded in 1874 that also favored women's suffrage

Nineteenth Amendment
Constitutional amendment ratified in 1920 that gave women the right to vote

Paul, Alice
Founder of the Congressional Union and the National Woman's Party

Rankin, Jeanette
The first woman elected to Congress, serving as a representative from Montana between 1917 and 1919 and also from 1941 to 1943

The Revolution
Suffragist newspaper published by Susan B. Anthony and Elizabeth Cady Stanton in the late 1860s and early 1870s

Rose, Ernestine
Jewish American women's rights activist in the mid-1800s

Second Great Awakening
Religious revival that swept the United States in the early 1800s

Shaw, Anna Howard
President of the National American Woman Suffrage Association in the early 1900s

Stanton, Elizabeth Cady
Women's suffrage pioneer who headed the National Woman's Suffrage Association (NWSA) and the National American Woman Suffrage Association (NAWSA)

Stone, Lucy
Women's suffrage pioneer who headed the American Woman Suffrage Association (AWSA)

Susan B. Anthony Amendment
An early name given to the constitutional amendment that eventually became the Nineteenth Amendment, which granted women the right to vote

Terrell, Mary Church
President of the National Association of Colored Women and an advocate for women's suffrage

Thirteenth Amendment
Constitutional amendment that outlawed slavery; ratified in 1865

Tilton, Theodore
Newspaper publisher who served as president of the National Woman's Suffrage Association in the early 1870s

Train, George Francis
Women's rights activist of the mid-1800s who became notorious for his racist statements against African Americans

Truth, Sojourner
African American abolitionist and women's rights activist in the mid-1800s

Wells-Barnett, Ida B.
African American suffragist and civil rights activist who was active from the 1890s through the 1920s

Willard, Frances
Leader of the National Women's Christian Temperance Union who promoted women's suffrage in the late 1800s

Woodhull, Victoria C.
Controversial women's rights activist who ran for president in 1872, 1880, and 1892

Wollstonecraft, Mary
 Eighteenth-century British author and women's rights advocate

Women's Convention
 A subgroup of the National Baptist Convention that promoted women's suffrage among African Americans beginning in the 1890s

Woman's Journal
 Suffragist newspaper published by Lucy Stone, Henry Blackwell, and Alice Stone Blackwell from the 1870s through the 1910s

CHRONOLOGY

1840

June 1840 – Lucretia Mott and Elizabeth Cady Stanton are among the American women who travel to London to attend the World Anti-Slavery Conference. After being prevented from taking part in the proceedings because of their sex, Mott and Stanton vow to hold a women's rights convention in the United States. *See* p. 15.

1848

July 19-20, 1848 – The Seneca Falls Woman's Rights Convention takes place in western New York State. *See* p. 17.

August 2, 1848 – A second convention takes place in Rochester, New York. *See* p. 19.

1850

April 19-20, 1850 – A women's convention is held in Salem, Ohio. *See* p. 22

October 23-24, 1850 – The first National Woman's Rights Convention is held in Worcester, Massachusetts. *See* p. 22.

1852

September 8-10, 1852 – The third National Woman's Rights Convention takes place in Syracuse, New York; Susan B. Anthony joins the suffrage movement at this event. *See* p. 24.

1854

Massachusetts becomes the first state to reform its property-rights laws, giving women more control over their money and property. Other states soon follow. *See* p. 27.

1861

April 12, 1861 – Confederate troops fire on Fort Sumter in Charleston, South Carolina, beginning the Civil War. Women's rights groups suspend their activities. *See* p. 29.

1863

May 14, 1863 – Women's rights activists form the National Woman's Loyal League. *See* p. 30.

1865

April 9, 1865 – General Robert E. Lee surrenders to General Ulysses S. Grant, ending the Civil War.

April 14, 1865 – President Lincoln is assassinated.

December 18, 1865 – The Thirteenth Amendment is added to the United States Constitution, outlawing slavery. *See* p. 30.

1866

May 10, 1866 – The American Equal Rights Association is formed, dedicated to upholding the rights of both African Americans and women. *See* p. 33.

June 1866 – Both houses of Congress approve the Fourteenth Amendment, which calls for a strengthening of African American voting rights but makes no provision for women's suffrage. *See* p. 33.

1867

November 1867 – Kansas holds a referendum on women's suffrage. Despite intense campaigning by women's rights activists, the measure is defeated. *See* p. 34.

1868

January 1868 – The first edition of *The Revolution,* a newspaper published by Susan B. Anthony and Elizabeth Cady Stanton, appears. *See* p. 35.

July 28, 1868 – The Fourteenth Amendment becomes part of the Constitution. *See* p. 36.

November and December 1868– Congress drafts and considers a Fifteenth Amendment stating that the right to vote cannot be denied "on account of race, color, or previous condition of servitude." *See* p. 36.

1869

January 19, 1869 – Elizabeth Cady Stanton calls for Sixteenth Amendment giving women the right to vote. *See* p. 36.

May 1869 – A tumultuous meeting of the American Equal Rights Association divides the suffragists into two camps. Soon after, a group led by Elizabeth Cady Stanton and Susan B. Anthony forms the rival National Woman's Suffrage Association (NWSA). *See* p. 38.

August 1869 – Lucy Stone and other activists form the American Woman Suffrage Association (AWSA) *See* p. 38.

December 10, 1869 – Wyoming Territory grants women the right to vote. *See* p. 47.

1870

February 10, 1870 – Utah Territory approves women's suffrage. *See* p. 47.

March 30, 1870 –The Fifteenth Amendment becomes part of the Constitution. *See* p. 38.

April 1870 – Victoria C. Woodhull announces that she is a candidate for the presidency of the United States. *See* p. 43.

1871

January 1871 – Woodhull addresses the House and Senate judiciary committees in Washington, D.C., arguing that women already have the right to vote. *See* p. 43.

1872

April 1872 – Susan B. Anthony prevents the NWSA from formally linking itself to Woodhull's Equal Rights Party. *See* p. 45.

November 1872 – After Woodhull's campaign falls apart, her newspaper publishes a story alleging that former AWSA president Henry Ward Beecher engaged in an adulterous affair. Woodhull and her sister are arrested for sending obscenity through the mail. *See* p. 46.

November 5, 1872 – Women across the country test the election laws by attempting to vote. Susan B. Anthony is among those arrested after she successfully votes in Rochester, New York. *See* p. 48.

1875

March 29, 1875 – In *Minor vs. Happersett,* the Supreme Court rules that the Fourteenth and Fifteenth Amendments do not give women the right to vote. *See* p. 50.

1878

A new draft amendment calling for women's suffrage is introduced in the United States Senate. It later becomes known as the Susan B. Anthony Amendment. *See* p. 51.

1883

November 1883 – Washington Territory grants women the right to vote. *See* p. 50.

1887

A Supreme Court ruling takes the vote away from women in Washington Territory, and an act of Congress does the same in Utah. *See* p. 50.

January 25, 1887 – The Susan B. Anthony Amendment fails to gain passage in the U.S. Senate, with 16 votes in favor, 34 against, and 25 abstentions. *See* p. 52.

1890

The National Woman's Suffrage Association (NWSA) and the American Woman Suffrage Association (AWSA) agree to merge, forming the National American Woman Suffrage Association (NAWSA). Elizabeth Cady Stanton becomes the first president of the united organization. *See* p. 53.

Wyoming becomes a state and continues to allow women the right to vote.

1892

Susan B. Anthony succeeds Stanton as NAWSA president. *See* p. 54.

1893

November 1893 – Colorado approves a women's suffrage referendum. *See* p. 54.

1895

Elizabeth Cady Stanton published the first volume of *The Woman's Bible. See* p. 59.

1896

January 1896 – A resolution is passed at the NAWSA convention disavowing any connection to Stanton's book. *See* p. 59.

The National Association of Colored Women is founded and immediately supports women's suffrage. *See* p. 58.

Utah becomes a state and its women regain the right to vote. *See* p. 60.

Women win the right to vote in Idaho. *See* p. 60.

1900

Susan B. Anthony resigns as president of NAWSA and is succeeded by Carrie Chapman Catt. *See* p. 60.

1902

October 26, 1902 – Elizabeth Cady Stanton dies at age eighty-seven. *See* p. 60.

1904

Anna Howard Shaw succeeds Carrie Chapman Catt as NAWSA president. *See* p. 60.

1906

March 13, 1906 – Susan B. Anthony dies at age eighty-six. *See* p. 60.

1907

Harriot Stanton Blatch forms the Equality League of Self-Supporting Women, which is dedicated to promoting suffrage among working-class women. *See* p. 66.

1910

The state of Washington passes a referendum giving women the right to vote. *See* p. 67.

1912

Women in Arizona, California, Kansas, and Oregon gain the right to vote. *See* p. 67.

December 1912 – Alice Paul arrives in Washington, D.C., to begin lobbying Congress for passage of the Susan B. Anthony amendment. *See* p. 69.

1913

March 3, 1913 – A suffrage parade organized by Alice Paul's Congressional Union brings 8,000 marchers to Washington, D.C. *See* p. 69.

1914

March 19, 1914 – The Susan B. Anthony Amendment fails to gain passage in the U.S. Senate; the tally—35 votes in favor and 34 against—falls well short of the necessary two-thirds majority.

August 2, 1914 – The German army invades Luxembourg, beginning World War I.

Montana and Nevada grant women the vote. *See* p. 68.

The Congressional Union separates from NAWSA and campaigns against Democratic congressional candidates, contributing to a number of Republican wins in the November elections. *See* p. 70.

1915

January 12, 1915 – The Susan B. Anthony Amendment fails in the U.S. House of Representatives by a vote of 174 votes in favor, 204 against.

December 1915 – Ann Howard Shaw resigns as NAWSA president and is succeeded by Carrie Chapman Catt. *See* p. 70.

1916

June 1916 – Alice Paul and her colleagues form the National Woman's Party (NWP). In the following months they once again campaign against the Democrats, including President Wilson. *See* p. 71.

September 1916 – Carrie Chapman Catt reveals her "Winning Plan" at a NAWSA meeting in Atlantic City, New Jersey. *See* p. 72.

November 7, 1916 – Democrat Woodrow Wilson is reelected to a second term as president. *See* p. 75.

1917

January 10, 1917 – Female protestors from the National Woman's Party begin picketing the White House to protest President Wilson's position on women's suffrage. *See* p. 77.

April 6, 1917 – The United States declares war on Germany. *See* p. 77.

June 22, 1917 – The first White House protesters are arrested. *See* p. 79.

August 1917 – Rioting takes place at the White House gates as counter-protestors and police battle the NWP picketers. *See* p. 80.

October 20, 1917 – Imprisoned NWP members begin hunger strikes at the Occuquan Workhouse. *See* p. 80.

November 6, 1917 – Voters in the state of New York grant women the right to vote. *See* p. 84.

November 27-28, 1917 – All suffrage protesters are released from jail. *See* p. 85.

1918

January 10, 1918 – The Susan B. Anthony Amendment is passed by a two-thirds majority in the U.S. House of Representative, 274 votes in favor, 136 against. *See* p. 86.

October 1, 1918 – The Susan B. Anthony Amendment fails to gain passage in the U.S. Senate; the tally—62 votes in favor, 34 against—again falls short of the necessary two-thirds majority. *See* p. 86.

November 5, 1918 – Women gain the ballot in Michigan, Oklahoma, and South Dakota. *See* p. 68.

November 11, 1918 – The Armistice goes into effect, ending World War I.

1919

February 10, 1919 – The Susan B. Anthony Amendment once again narrowly fails to gain the necessary two-thirds majority for passage in the U.S. Senate, with 63 senators voting in favor and 33 voting against.

May 21, 1919 – The Susan B. Anthony Amendment is once again approved by the U.S. House of Representative, 304 votes in favor, 89 against. *See* p. 87.

June 4, 1919 – The Susan B. Anthony Amendment is passed by a two-thirds majority in the U.S. Senate, with 56 votes in favor and 25 votes against. *See* p. 87.

June 10, 1919 – Michigan and Wisconsin become the first states to ratify the Nineteenth Amendment. *See* p. 88.

1920

August 18, 1920 – Tennessee becomes the thirty-sixth state to ratify the Nineteenth Amendment. *See* p. 89.

August 26, 1920 – The Nineteenth Amendment officially becomes part of the United States Constitution, giving women throughout the country the right to vote. *See* p. 90.

NARRATIVE OVERVIEW

PROLOGUE

On a July morning in 1848, four women stood outside of the Wesleyan Chapel in Seneca Falls, New York. They had called a meeting at the church, but upon arriving they found the door locked. Perhaps they found it fitting that they were left standing outside. After all, the purpose of their gathering was to discuss how women were being left out of some of the most important aspects of American society, including education, justice, and the democratic process.

They had outlined the purpose of the meeting in a brief advertisement that had run in the *Seneca County Courier* several days earlier:

> Woman's Rights Convention.—A Convention to discuss the social, civil, and religious condition and rights of women, will be held in the Wesleyan Chapel at Seneca Falls, N.Y., on Wednesday and Thursday, the 19th and 20th of July, concurrent; commencing at 10 o'clock A.M. During the first day the meeting will be exclusively for women, who are earnestly invited to attend. The public generally are invited to be present on the second day, when Lucretia Mott, of Philadelphia, and other ladies and gentlemen, will address the convention.

The announcement sounded innocent enough, yet even these few words marked the Seneca Falls gathering as very unusual for its time. In the mid-1800s, public debate over the role of women in American society was very rare, and it was even more rare for women themselves to be part of the discussion. In fact, very few women spoke in public at this time. Of the four women who had called the Seneca Falls meeting, only one had any experience in speaking before a large group. Many people considered it somewhat shocking for women to attend a politically oriented gathering, let alone organize such a meeting and direct the discussion.

Yet there they stood in front of the locked chapel doors: Lucretia Mott, Elizabeth Cady Stanton, Martha C. Wright, and Mary Ann McClintock. They were soon joined by 300 other people—men and women—who had heeded that call. And before them was a locked door. Luckily, it did not stay locked for long. A member of the group hoisted a child through a window to unbolt the door and allow the crowd to enter.

Over the course of the next two days, the women's suffrage movement was born. When the Seneca Falls Convention set down its list of resolutions, one of them became the rallying point that would drive a nationwide campaign: "That it is the duty of the women of this country to secure to themselves their sacred right to the elective franchise." In plainer terms, it was their duty to win the right to vote.

Winning that fight would take more than 70 years of hard work. In that time, prominent new suffragists would join the movement, and others would leave it. Activists would battle against a wide array of opponents, and they would also fight amongst themselves. Eventually, all of the movement's pioneers would die before achieving their goal. The fight would be carried on by their daughters, both real and figurative, and in some cases by their granddaughters.

It seems doubtful that the women who organized the Seneca Falls meeting fully understood the magnitude of the task that lay before them. In the declaration that they presented to the convention, however, they anticipated some of the challenges they would face and expressed determination to overcome them:

> In entering the great work before us, we anticipate no small amount of misconception, misrepresentation, and ridicule; but we shall use every instrumentality within our power to effect our object.

Chapter One

THE ORIGINS OF THE WOMEN'S SUFFRAGE MOVEMENT

I ask no favors for my sex. All I ask of our brethren is that they take their feet from off our necks and permit us to stand upright on the ground which God has deigned us to occupy.

—Sarah Grimké, *Letters on the Equality of the Sexes, and the Condition of Woman,* 1838

Though the initial call for women's suffrage did not occur until the mid-1800s, many earlier events set the stage for the Seneca Falls Convention. To understand the debate over gender and democracy in America, it is helpful to look at the way people lived and voted in the two centuries after Europeans first landed on the east coast of North America.

Because the area that eventually became the United States of America was largely settled by English colonists, many British customs of law and government were transferred to North America. Voting was one of these customs. British law placed numerous restrictions on voting rights. In general, voting was limited to adult white men who owned property, although practices varied somewhat in the different colonies. For instance, certain colonies defined "property" as land and buildings, while others defined it more broadly to include all personal property, such as livestock or other items of a certain value. In a few places in Massachusetts and New York, the emphasis on property ownership as the determining factor in voting rights gave selected women the right to vote. These women were usually widows who had inherited property from their deceased husbands. Aside from these few exceptions, however, women were not allowed to have a voice in the electoral process.

British legal scholar Sir William Blackstone influenced women's rights in the American colonies with his opinion that "by marriage the husband and wife are one person in law."

The exclusion of women stemmed from a variety of factors, but the most important one was the social role that women fulfilled in the 1600s and 1700s. The majority of women were engaged as mothers and homemakers, and English Common Law defined them in this way. Rather than being seen as individuals with certain rights, they were viewed as part of their family or household, which was normally headed by a man. *The Lawes Resolutions of Women's Rights; or, the Lawes Provisions for Women*, a legal text published in 1632, addresses the status of a married woman, stating that "her companion" (that is, her husband) is "her master." The book also proclaims that "women have no voice in Parliament. They make no laws, they consent to none, they abrogate [abolish] none."

While this system certainly gave preference to men, it did not totally ignore women. Instead, the law assumed that a woman's rights would be protected or "covered" by her husband—a concept known as "coverture." This concept became more firmly established in the legal code thanks to the influential British legal authority Sir William Blackstone. In his book *Commentaries on the Laws of England*, published in 1765, Blackstone stated that "by marriage the husband and wife are one person in law; that is, the very being or legal existence of the woman is suspended during the marriage, or at least incorporated and consolidated into that of the husband; under whose wing, protection and cover she performs everything."

This idea of consolidating the legal interests of husbands and wives was carried over to voting. In the opinion of most political authorities of the 1600s and 1700s, the only person who should be allowed to cast a ballot was the head of the household—a man. Some people argued that women could not be allowed to vote because they were not independent enough to express their own free will. Since most women were economically dependent upon their husbands, it was widely assumed that men would control women's votes. Therefore, some people opposed granting women the right to vote because they believed that this action would actually give greater political power to married men. This same idea was used to justify restricting the vote to property owners. Many people believed that those who did not own property were likely to be influenced by wealthier figures in the community, who had the power to grant jobs and other favors to the less affluent.

The social status and legal treatment of women in the seventeenth and eighteenth centuries was also grounded in the traditions of Western civilization. Because the people of Europe and the North American colonies were primarily Christian, many of them looked to the Bible for their understanding of the relationship between men and women and between women and society as a whole. The story of Adam and Eve from Genesis, the first book of the Old Testament, was often upheld as proof of the inferior status of women. After Eve is beguiled by serpent and eats the forbidden fruit, the Lord God decrees that "your desire shall be for your husband, and he shall rule over you." This passage would be recited again and again by opponents of women's suffrage.

These legal and religious influences produced a society that placed women in a decidedly inferior position to men. For instance, a married woman could not own property. Instead, any land or goods that she held prior to marriage or inherited after marriage belonged to her husband. If a married woman worked, her wages legally went to her spouse. Separation and divorce were quite rare compared with modern times, but when these situations occurred, men received preferential treatment. The children of divorcing parents, for example, usually came under custody of the father.

One of the most frustrating situations for women of the colonial era occurred when a woman owned property or inherited it after her husband died. In such cases, the women were liable for the taxes on the property. But since women were unable to vote, they had no voice in how the government used the tax money. This sort of "taxation without representation" became one of the key issues that inspired the American colonies to seek independence from Great Britain. The colonists objected to the British government's practice of taxing them without allowing them to elect representatives to promote their interests within the government. Despite the fact that widespread disapproval of taxation without representation played a role in the American Revolution, however, the successful fight for independence did not provide relief to women. Even in the newly formed United States, women continued to be taxed even as they remained blocked from voting or participating in other fundamental elements of the political process.

The strict social roles of the eighteenth century proved just as confining for women as the legal code. Girls and women enjoyed few opportunities to obtain an education or employment outside the home. Instead, they were expected to fill their days with household chores, child care, and churchly duties. Church was one of the few places where meaningful interaction with men outside their immediate family was socially acceptable, but even here they were expected to yield to the opposite sex on all matters of consequence. Indeed, social norms discouraged women from voicing their opinions in public—especially when men were present.

Revolutionary Ideas

The revolutionaries who advocated American independence from Great Britain in the 1760s and 1770s were inspired by a variety of ideas, but two were of particular importance to the issue of women's rights and suffrage. As plainly stated in the most famous passage of the Declaration of Independence, the rebellious colonists maintained that "all men are created equal" and that governments receive their "just powers from the consent of the governed." If the term "all men" is taken to mean all of mankind, these points seem to suggest that the American patriots may have wanted to give women a greater voice in the political process. Yet, in this regard, most of the Founding Fathers held a rather limited view of equality and gave little consideration to including women's voices in the new government they were creating. In terms of immediate changes, therefore, the American Revolution had little effect on women's rights, especially their right to vote. When the colonies became independent states, they made very few changes in their voting practices in regard to women.

But when the larger picture is considered, American independence can be viewed as an important step in the march toward women's suffrage. The creation of the new nation inspired a general atmosphere of liberal change that extended well into the 1800s, when the campaign for women's rights began in earnest. With its emphasis on personal liberty, the American Revolution was a triumph of individualism and inspired a prolonged debate over the "natural rights" that belonged to each person. There were many who saw vot-

The signing of the Declaration of Independence in 1776 did little to increase the rights of American women.

ing as one of those rights. In time, a large group of people would claim that right for women as well as men.

One of the most famous pleas for improved treatment of women was uttered in the midst of the revolutionary era. Abigail Adams, wife of patriot and future president John Adams, wrote a letter to her husband in March 1776, as he was taking part in the Continental Congress in Philadelphia. In it, she offers her husband some frank advice in drafting the laws of the new country:

> I desire you would remember the ladies and be more favorable to them than your ancestors. Do not put such unlimited power into the hands of husbands. Remember all men would be tyrants if they could. If particular care and attention are not paid to the ladies, we are determined to foment [launch] a rebellion and will not hold ourselves bound to obey any laws in which we have no voice or representation.

Future First Lady Abigail Adams believed that the newly formed United States government should grant women the right to vote.

As it turned out, Abigail Adams's suggestions did not have much impact on her husband. "As to your extraordinary code of laws," he wrote in reply, "I cannot help but laugh." Indeed, John Adams would prove to be one of the more conservative of Founding Fathers when it came to voting rights. When other politicians proposed easing property restrictions so that more Americans could vote, Adams opposed the measures. "It is dangerous to open so fruitful a source of controversy and altercation as would be opened by attempting to alter the qualifications of voters," he wrote in 1776. "There will be no end of it. New claims will arise; women will demand the vote."

Adams's prediction was premature, as concerted efforts to promote women's suffrage did not begin for several decades. But a detailed condemnation of the second-class status of women in both the United States and England was not far off. In 1792 the English author Mary Wollstonecraft published her highly influential book *A Vindication of the Rights of Women*. Although it did not specifically take up the subject of voting rights, the book had an immense influence on the suffrage activists who came later. In fact, it presented many of the basic concepts of gender equality that would inspire the feminist movement almost two centuries later.

Among its other messages, Wollstonecraft's book asserted that women and men shared a similar nature and possessed a similar capacity to develop their "abilities and virtues." Wollstonecraft conceded that, on the whole, the intellectual development of women lagged behind that of men at the time of her writing. But she blamed this on the fact that women were "treated as a kind of subordinate beings, and not as part of the human species." Wollstonecraft also railed against society's tendency to treat women as alluring sexual objects instead of capable individuals, thereby denying them opportunities for education and intellectual fulfillment.

Democracy in the New Nation

As the American states formed new governments following independence, the issue of voting rights—specifically, who would be allowed to vote—created controversy. As in the colonial era, different areas developed different regulations. Some of the new states kept their old, colonial rules in place—limiting the vote to property owners, for instance. But others embraced the liberal ideals expressed in the Declaration of Independence with more enthusiasm. Pennsylvania eliminated all property requirements in 1776, giving the vote to all men who paid taxes. Vermont went even further in 1777, tossing out both property and taxpaying requirements, which in effect allowed all free men to vote.

Author Mary Wollstonecraft presented some of the earliest feminist arguments in her influential 1792 book *A Vindication of the Rights of Women.*

But enfranchising women (that is, giving them the right to vote) was rarely even considered. In fact, women achieved the right to vote in only one state during the 1700s. Prior to 1790, New Jersey laws had granted "all free inhabitants" the right to vote. Although this terminology might have been interpreted to mean that women could cast ballots, few people took it that way. Such "gender-neutral" language was used in other states as well, but almost no one believed that the word "all" included women. In 1790, however, the New Jersey state legislature amended its election laws, inserting the phrase "he or she" to refer to voters. New Jersey's use of the term "he or she" removed any doubt about who was enfranchised.

New Jersey's election laws did not cause an immediate stir. They became an issue in 1797, however, when a group of women in Elizabethtown joined

The Quakers: Agents of Change

While many Christian groups in the 1700s and 1800s imposed strict limitations on women's activities, the Religious Society of Friends— better known as the Quakers—proved much more liberal. Founded in England by George Fox in 1652, the group was known for its plain dress, lack of a formal religious clergy, and opposition to war. From the beginning, the group promoted equality between the sexes, allowing women to lead worship services and to have a voice in community affairs. The Quakers also tended to be ardent reformers. In fact, its members led some of the earliest anti-slavery protests in North America.

The Quakers proved extremely important in launching the fight for women's rights. Many pioneers of the suffrage movement belonged to the Society of Friends or had previously been members, including Sarah and Angelina Grimké, Lucretia Mott, and Susan B. Anthony. Though Elizabeth Cady Stanton was not a member of the church, the *History of Woman Suffrage* notes that she found "the most congenial associations in Quaker families." Decades later, a Quaker woman named Alice Paul helped win passage of the amendment that finally gave women the right to vote. The connection between Quakerism and suffrage was far from accidental. According to Quaker theology, every person possesses the "Inner Light" of the "Divine Spirit." This idea matched the growing trend toward individualism that led to greater political rights for women and others.

together to oppose a legislative candidate, and their votes almost swung the election to his opponent. Male politicians grew worried about women acting together to form a powerful political coalition, and they launched a campaign to repeal female voting rights. This effort succeeded in 1807, aided by charges that women had engaged in illegal voting practices.

Meanwhile, the right to vote expanded to include more and more American men during the early nineteenth century. By the 1850s, all of the property requirements for voting had been abolished. Some states retained or introduced guidelines that required voters to be taxpayers, but this limitation also became increasingly rare by the mid-1800s. In addition, recently arrived immigrants were allowed to vote in many places, especially in western frontier territories eager to attract settlers.

There were a variety of reasons why the old limitations on voting rights were cast aside. First, the values of liberty and equality (at least for white male citizens) became more entrenched throughout the country, and this attitude was reflected in more liberal election laws. Second, it became less common for Americans to own land in the early 1800s. If property requirements had not been eased, the percentage of the public allowed to vote would have decreased, undermining the nation's growing identity as a place of liberty and justice. Finally, the growth of political parties helped open the polls to larger numbers of people. As the different political groups sought to gain an advantage over their rivals, they frequently eased voting restrictions, hoping to draw more voters to their party.

Despite the lifting of some voting restrictions, however, there were still many classes of people that could not vote. Women and African-American slaves were excluded from voting everywhere. Free blacks, Native Americans, and other minorities were barred from the polls in many places, though not all. Nonetheless, the spread of democracy among the white male population created favorable conditions for the women's suffrage movement. As more and more citizens were allowed to cast ballots, it became increasingly difficult to exclude others.

Religion and Reform

Many cultural changes were taking place in the United States in the early 1800s that also contributed to the spread of voting rights. One of the most important of these changes was the religious revival known as the Second Great Awakening, which reached its peak in the 1830s (the First Great Awakening had taken place a century earlier). The movement reflected a major change in religious ideas. Previously, the Calvinist tradition had maintained that salvation rested largely in God's hands. The Second Great Awakening placed more emphasis on the individual, promoting the idea that people could take an active role in achieving their own salvation by accepting God, turning away from sin, and atoning for any transgressions already committed.

During the Second Great Awakening, large religious revivals and camp meetings took place all across the country. These gatherings proved especially

The abolition movement produced seasoned activists like sisters Angelina and Sarah Grimké, who later turned their attention to women's suffrage.

attractive to women, who attended in large numbers. The leaders of these meetings commonly appealed to the attendees to choose God and convert to Christianity. By focusing on personal choice and individual action, the Second Great Awakening helped reinforce the idea that people had the power to bring about important changes. This attitude would be a major inspiration to the activists who took up the battle for women's suffrage.

Before that campaign could begin, however, two other causes took center stage: temperance and abolition. Both the movement to eliminate alcohol consumption and the movement to end slavery were closely related to the Second Great Awakening. The religious revival stressed the need to fight against sin, and many activists identified excessive alcohol consumption and slavery as national sins that needed to be vanquished. The suffragists who came later were influenced by both of these reform movements, but they drew their largest inspiration from the fight against slavery. In a sense, abolition became the launching pad for the women's rights movement.

Although the leading abolitionists were men, the movement also attracted large numbers of women. Since many of them had never before taken a public role, the crusade against slavery became a sort of training camp where they learned the basics of political activism and organization. Perhaps more importantly, women abolitionists learned to speak out in public before mixed gatherings that included men and women. (Such gatherings were referred to as "promiscuous audiences" at the time.) Taking such a prominent role in a public debate was a very controversial thing for a woman to do in the early 1800s. It was even more controversial for women to champion abolition—which was regarded as the most radical concept of the time.

Female activists in the abolitionist movement sometimes faced violent opposition. For example, a group of protesters burst into an 1835 meeting of the Boston Female Anti-Slavery Society, forcing the women to flee. A similar scene took place in Philadelphia in 1838, when a meeting of the Anti-Slavery Convention of American Women was disrupted by opponents who set fire to the hall after the women had departed.

Opposition to female activists also came from inside the anti-slavery movement. In 1836 and 1837, sisters Sarah and Angelina Grimké made a series of speeches against slavery in New York and New England. Conservative abolitionists opposed the talks because they felt that women had no business speaking in public. The controversy did not deter the Grimkés, though, and actually helped them to better understand the unfair conditions faced by women. In 1838 Sarah Grimké published *Letters on the Equality of the Sexes, and the Condition of Woman*, which pointed out similarities between the legal status of women and that of slaves.

The dispute about the proper role of women in the abolitionist movement reached a peak in 1840, when William Lloyd Garrison—one of the nation's most prominent anti-slavery activists—appointed Abby Kelly (later Abby Kelly Foster) to the business committee of the American Anti-Slavery Society. This appointment caused a major rift in the organization, as many men opposed having a woman in a leadership position. A month later, a mixed group of male and female abolitionists traveled to the World Anti-Slavery Convention in London. At this event, conservative men in the American delegation were able to prevent the women from fully participating in the meeting. Instead, the women were confined to a corner of the hall where they could not be seen or heard.

At the London Anti-Slavery Convention of 1840, women were segregated from men and not allowed to speak. This bitter experience provided the spark for the women's suffrage movement.

It was a bitter experience for the women, as well as for some of their male colleagues who opposed the ban. But it also provided the spark that eventually ignited the women's suffrage movement. Among the women at the conference were 25-year-old Elizabeth Cady Stanton and 47-year-old Lucretia Mott (see biographies on Stanton, p. 125, and Mott, p. 119). The two women became fast friends during the conference and spent many hours discussing the status of women in American society. They agreed upon the need to hold a convention to promote women's rights when they returned to the United States. Although eight years passed before Stanton and Mott once again sat down together to discuss the issues they had first considered in London, the two women ultimately kept their vow.

Chapter Two

THE BEGINNING OF CHANGE

For those who do not yet understand the real objects of our recent Conventions at Rochester and Seneca Falls, I would state that we did not meet to discuss fashions, customs, or dress, the rights or duties of man, nor the propriety of the sexes changing positions, but simply our own inalienable rights.

—Elizabeth Cady Stanton, *National Reformer*, September 14, 1848

The historic Women's Rights Convention that took place in Seneca Falls, New York, in July 1848 actually came about somewhat by chance. One of its organizers, Lucretia Mott, had traveled from her home in Philadelphia to western New York to attend a Quaker meeting and visit her sister, Martha C. Wright. During her stay, Mott was reunited with Elizabeth Cady Stanton, the young woman she had met in London eight years earlier. Stanton had only moved to Seneca Falls the year before. Immediately after resuming their acquaintance, Mott and Stanton started organizing the women's rights convention that they had discussed in London. They put together a rough blueprint for the gathering in a matter of days.

Three days before the meeting, Stanton and Mott sat down with Wright and Mary Ann McClintock to draft a declaration of purpose and a series of resolutions for the convention to consider. As described in *History of Woman Suffrage*, the women initially felt overwhelmed by the task, "as helpless and hopeless as if they had suddenly been asked to construct a steam engine." Then someone came up with the idea of looking at declarations that had been previously published. The group eventually located a copy of the Declaration of

One of the organizers of the Seneca Falls Convention, Elizabeth Cady Stanton, with her daughter Harriot, who became a suffrage activist in adulthood.

Independence, the historic 1776 document that had declared the American colonies an independent nation, separate from Great Britain. After reading the declaration aloud, the women "at once decided to adopt the historic document, with some slight changes." The most significant change involved clarifying author Thomas Jefferson's basic plea for equality so that it applied to both sexes: "We hold these truths to be self-evident: that all men and women are created equal." In this way, the document that had inspired American independence was used to launch another revolution.

The area around Seneca Falls was home to a large number of Quakers and other progressive activists, and the women's rights convention was well attended. But the audience that packed the Wesleyan Chapel did not necessarily support the idea of giving women the right to vote. The resolution calling for the "elective franchise" was just one of many proposed reforms, and it was by far the most controversial (see "Declaration of Sentiments and Resolutions, 1848 Seneca Falls Convention," p. 151). Stanton had added the suffrage resolution over the objections of Mott. "Oh Lizzie!," Mott said to Stanton. "If thou demands that, thou will make us ridiculous! We must go slowly." Stanton's husband also opposed the idea, and when Elizabeth refused to give up the call for suffrage, he boycotted the convention.

During the two days of the convention, however, Stanton gained support for her resolution from several influential figures. One was Frederick Douglass, the former slave who became a famous abolition leader and writer. When the attendees voted on the resolutions at the end of convention, they approved the call for suffrage by a very narrow margin. All of the other resolutions passed unanimously.

Yᵉ MAY SESSION OF Yᵉ WOMAN'S RIGHTS CONVENTION—Yᵉ ORATOR OF Yᵉ DAY DENOUNCING Yᵉ LORDS OF CREATION.

A cartoon drawing from *Harper's Weekly* depicting the Seneca Falls Convention.

At the close of Seneca Falls meeting, the attendees decided that they needed more time to discuss the subjects they had raised. They held a second convention two weeks later in Rochester, New York, and it turned out to be even larger than the first. The women at this gathering demonstrated that they were already gaining confidence. During the first meeting, they had relied on James Mott, Lucretia's husband, to chair the discussion. But in Rochester they put a woman, Abigail Bush, in charge of the proceedings. According to the *History of Woman Suffrage*, "the calm way she assumed the duties of the office, and the admirable manner in which she discharged them, soon reconciled the opposition to the seemingly ridiculous experiment." Some of the other women who tried to speak at the meeting had less success, however, suffering from "trembling frames and faltering tongues."

The Rochester convention adjourned with another set of resolutions. Several of the measures stressed economic inequities, such as laws preventing married women from owning and inheriting property, for example, and the

The Blooming of Bloomers

THE BLOOMER COSTUME.

The bloomer costume

The standard female outfit of the mid-1800s was impractical, uncomfortable, and unhealthy. It consisted of a large, hoop-skirt dress, multiple layers of petticoats, and restrictive bodices and stays that squeezed the torso into an idealized hourglass shape. Beginning in the 1850s, mavericks in the United States rebelled against this conventional style and adopted a type of pants outfit that had originated in Europe. Sometimes called pantelettes and pantaloons, this attire became better known as "the Bloomer outfit," or simply "bloomers," after the temperance activist Amelia Bloomer, who helped popularize the style.

The pants, often worn under a knee-length skirt, became a symbol of liberation for women of the era. Several suffrage figures sported bloomers for a time, including Elizabeth Cady Stanton, Lucy Stone, and Susan B. Anthony. "What a liberty I felt, in running up and down stairs with my hands free to carry whatsoever I would," Stanton said after putting on her pantelettes. But controversy came with the comfort. Stanton noted that "people would stare" when she wore her bloomers, and that "men and women make rude remarks; boys follow in crowds, or shout from behind fences." Anthony concluded that the outfit was "a physical comfort but a mental crucifixion" because of the torment she was subjected to while wearing it. Many of the women's rights pioneers gave up their bloomers after a few years, as did most other women, but the style made a resurgence in the late 1800s, as women became more physically active.

levying of taxes on working women even though they did not have a voice in government. Once again, however, the most controversial of the convention resolutions was the one calling for women's suffrage.

Shining a Spotlight on Women's Rights

The resolutions passed in Seneca Falls and Rochester had no legal standing. But the purpose of the conventions was not to make laws, but rather to focus public attention on women's rights and spur further action. The conventions proved very successful on both counts. The subject of women's rights was so unusual for the era that the conventions received coverage in newspapers far beyond western New York. In most cases, though, the media criticized or mocked the activists. "It requires no argument to prove that this all is wrong," stated an Albany paper, the *Mechanic's Advocate*, in its coverage of the conventions. "Every true hearted female will instantly feel that this is unwomanly." The *Philadelphia Public Ledger and Daily Transcript* scoffed at the idea that women should have any rights or responsibilities beyond those of wife and mother, asserting that "a woman is nobody. A wife is everything." The *Worcester Telegraph*, from Massachusetts, ridiculed the conventioneers by calling them "Amazons"—a reference to the tribe of powerful women from Greek mythology.

As these reactions indicate, the suffragists faced vocal opposition almost from the time they adjourned their first meeting. Over the years that followed, opponents put forth a variety of justifications for their resistance to enfranchising women (see "Francis Parkman Recounts Arguments Against Women's Suffrage," p. 175). Most importantly, opponents claimed that there were distinct differences between men and women. This theory did not necessarily contend that women were inferior, but rather argued that both God and nature had willed them to operate in the domestic sphere—to bear and raise children and maintain the home. If women were to enter the political arena, opponents argued, then their vital feminine qualities would be undermined. This, in turn, would threaten the basic family structure that American society rested upon. A delegate to the California constitutional convention in 1879 summed up these ideas by stating that women's suffrage "attacks the integrity of the family; it attacks the eternal decrees of God Almighty; it denies and repudiates the obligations of motherhood."

Some suffragists responded to these attacks by arguing that feminine input would actually improve politics rather than harm women. "When our mothers, wives, and sisters vote with us," stated one male suffragist, "we will have purer legislation and better execution of our laws." Nonetheless, the view that voting women represented a threat to the nation's basic social fabric was an obstacle that the women's rights activists would battle against for decades.

Not all of the media coverage of the New York conventions was negative. One of the most influential papers in the country, the *New York Tribune*, maintained that the women's rights meetings were "the assertion of a natural right and as such must be conceded." The paper's editor, Horace Greeley, would continue to support the cause of women's suffrage for the next two decades. In addition, many suffrage activists felt that any publicity about women's rights—whether positive or negative—helped the cause. While the *New York Herald* denounced the conventions, for instance, it also reprinted the Declaration of Sentiments from Seneca Falls. Elizabeth Cady Stanton was pleased that the *Herald* brought the resolutions to a wider audience. "It will start women thinking," she said, "and men too; and when men and women think about a new question, the first step in progress is taken."

Two additional conventions were held in 1850, one in Ohio and one in Massachusetts. The First National Woman's Rights Convention, which took place in Worcester, Massachusetts, was largely organized by new activists from New England. Several of them would soon join Stanton and Mott as the leading figures in the suffrage movement. Paulina Wright Davis, who served as the president of the convention, approached the issue of women's rights from a physical and medical perspective. Beginning in the late 1840s, she had presented lectures to women on the anatomy and functions of the female body, using a mannequin she had imported from France. This kind of information was so rare, and the sight of the nude mannequin so shocking, that some attendees fled the room or fainted, according to some accounts. The Worcester meeting also marked the first appearance of Lucy Stone at a suffrage convention (see biography of Stone, p. 129). Armed with a polished speaking style and a college education (which was extremely rare for a woman at that time), Stone made a big impression on the Worcester gathering. Her prestige grew in the years that followed, and her fame eventually equaled that of Elizabeth Cady Stanton.

Progressive Allies

The First National Woman's Rights Convention provided further evidence of the link between the women's rights and abolitionist movements. Frederick Douglass attended the Worcester meeting, as did such other prominent antislavery activists as William Lloyd Garrison and Abby Kelly Foster. The leading women's rights activists—including Stanton, Stone, and Mott—were also vocal opponents of slavery, and many activists split their time between the two causes. Another figure who promoted the rights of both women and African Americans was the former slave Sojourner Truth (see biography of Truth, p. xx). At an 1851 convention in Akron, Ohio, she delivered her famous "Ain't I a Woman" speech, in which she linked her plight as a slave with her existence as a woman (see "Sojourner Truth's 'A'n't I a Woman' Speech, " p. 156).

The abolitionist movement was a vital source of strength for the suffragists, because it allowed them to draw upon the pool of progressive activists who were fighting slavery. On the other hand, the suffragists also paid a price for the alliance. During the 1850s the issue of slavery gripped the nation like no other. Many of the women's rights advocates became so caught up in their abolition work that they could not devote much time to promoting suffrage and other feminist causes. In

Susan B. Anthony in 1852, the year she attended her first women's rights convention.

addition, the issues of African American rights and women's rights often came to be seen as competing with one another in the post-Civil War era. The resulting tempest between activists for the two causes further slowed the march toward women's suffrage.

Many suffrage activists also promoted social change through the temperance movement. The fight against alcohol consumption was especially appealing to women, because it was widely perceived that men most often abused alcohol, while their wives suffered the majority of the consequences. Once they had waded into activism, many temperance advocates broadened their focus to include the cause of women's rights. This was the course followed by the person who would prove to be the most enduring advocate of female suffrage—Susan B. Anthony (see biography of Anthony, p. 105). Anthony began working with the Daughters of Temperance in western New York in 1848. A few years later she helped form the New York State Temperance Society (Elizabeth Cady Stanton, who also promoted temperance, served as the society's president). Anthony formally entered feminist activism after she was denied the right to speak at several anti-alcohol meetings on the basis of her gender. In one case, she was told that "sisters were not invited to speak, but to listen and learn." Anthony rebelled against such attitudes by attending the Third National Woman's Rights Convention in Syracuse, New York, in 1852. This event marked the beginning of her lifelong crusade for women's suffrage.

As Anthony switched her energies from temperance to women's rights, she became a close colleague of Elizabeth Cady Stanton. The two women soon established a complementary working relationship that endured for decades. Stanton was an eloquent speaker and writer who furnished many of the ideas that powered the women's rights movement. But as a married woman raising a total of seven children, her free time was limited. In addition, Stanton was sometimes distracted from the central issue of suffrage by her interest in other issues related to women, including divorce and religious reform.

Anthony's strength lay in her organizational abilities. While she lacked Stanton's ability with words, she was practical, efficient, focused, dedicated, and knew how to get things done. Unmarried by choice, she was able to devote countless hours to the movement. Once Anthony took up the cause of suffrage, her life became consumed by travel, speeches, petition drives, lobbying, and fund-raising—as well as the task of giving Stanton a firm nudge when it was needed. "She has been my good angel," Stanton admitted, "always pushing and goading me to work." When the two women appeared together, it was always Stanton who claimed the limelight. But Anthony understood and accepted this arrangement. "I felt that our cause was most profited by [Stanton] being seen and heard," she said, "and my best work was making the way clear for her." Stanton explained their relationship in another way. "I forged the thunderbolts," she said, referring to her ideas and writing ability, "and [Anthony] fired them."

By the mid-1850s, several other figures had emerged as important leaders in the suffrage movement. Antoinette Brown (later Antoinette Brown Blackwell) became a spokesperson for devoutly Christian suffragists. Most of the early women's rights activists came from a religious background, but some—including Elizabeth Cady Stanton—had come to believe that the traditional male-oriented interpretations of Christianity hindered women's progress toward full citizenship. In contrast, Brown was a progressive female activist who wholeheartedly embraced religion. In 1853 she became the first woman in the United States to be ordained as a minister in a mainstream denomination (the Congregational Church). On the other side of the coin

24

The First Family of Women's Rights

Lucy Stone

A number of men played prominent roles in the fight for women's rights. Among them was Henry Blackwell, an abolitionist from Ohio who began advocating female rights in 1853. That same year he met Lucy Stone, one of the rising stars of the suffrage movement, and asked her to be his wife. Stone, like fellow activist Susan B. Anthony, had decided against marriage and turned him down. But Blackwell was persistent, and Stone eventually accepted his proposal.

Their marriage in 1855 served as a political statement as well as an exchange of wedding vows. The ceremony included a formal protest against existing marriage laws, and copies were distributed to the press. Even more shocking was the fact that Stone decided to keep her maiden name, which launched a feminist trend that has continued to the present. For decades afterward, women who opted not to adopt their husbands' surnames became known as "Lucy Stoners."

A year later, Henry Blackwell's brother Samuel married women's rights activist Antoinette Brown, who was Stone's close friend and former classmate at Oberlin College in Ohio (one of the few institutions of higher learning open to women at that time). In addition, this extended family of activists included Elizabeth Blackwell, Henry's sister, who was one of the first women in the United States to earn a medical degree, and—eventually—Alice Stone Blackwell, the daughter of Lucy and Henry, who took up the cause of suffrage when she became an adult.

was Ernestine Rose, a Jew who had immigrated to America from Poland. Like Stanton, Rose felt impatient with the Christian emphasis some activists brought to the movement. She maintained that reform should be based upon "human rights and freedom" and "the laws of humanity" rather than the teachings of the Bible.

Small-town Activism, 1851

In the early years of the women's rights movement, campaigners often had to do much more than make speeches. In the following excerpt, activist Frances Gage recalls the extraordinary demands of one speaking engagement:

In December of 1851 I was invited to attend a Woman's Rights Convention in the town of Mount Gilead, Morrow Co., Ohio.... I wrote I would be there. It was two days' journey by steamboat and rail.... When we got to the house, there was not one human soul on hand, no fire in the old rusty stove, and the rude, unpainted board benches, all topsy-turvy. I called some boys playing near, asked their names, put them on paper, five of them, and said to them, "Go to every house in this town and tell everybody that 'Aunt Fanny' will speak here at 11 A.M., and if you get me fifty to come and hear, I will give you each ten cents." They scattered off upon the run. I ordered John to right the benches, picked up chips and kindlings, borrowed a brand of fire at the next door, had a good hot stove, and the floor swept, and was ready for my audience at the appointed time. John had done his work well, and fifty at least were on hand, and a minister to make a prayer and quote St. Paul before I said a word. I said my say, and before 1 P.M., we adjourned, appointing another session at 3, and one for 7 P.M., and three for the following day. Mrs. C. M. Severance [another woman's rights advocate] came at 6 P.M., and we had a good meeting throughout.

Source: Frances D. Gage, "Women's Rights Meeting in a Barn—'John's Convention,'" *History of Woman Suffrage*, Vol. 1, edited by Elizabeth Cady Stanton, Susan B. Anthony, and Matilda Joslyn Gage. New York: Fowler & Wells, 1881.

Slow Progress

Women's rights activists continued to hold an annual convention throughout the 1850s. They also organized on the state and local levels, and it was at this level that the movement scored its most significant victories. Many of the advances concerned reforms of laws that governed a woman's right to control her own money and property. Many activists viewed property-rights reform as an important first step toward greater equality. In the words of Susan B. Anthony, a "woman must have a purse of her own" in order to begin improving her condition.

Property-rights statutes in the United States were matters of state rather than federal law, so the changes had to be won on a state-by-state basis. Activists traveled hundreds of miles collecting signatures on petitions that called for revision of existing state laws governing property rights. In 1854 Massachusetts became the first state to enact such a reform, and other states soon followed suit. Anthony and Stanton led the fight in New York, which amended its laws in 1860. As the laws changed in state after state, women achieved a new legal status across the United States. Women gained the right to own property independently, and Blackstone's concept that "by marriage the husband and wife are one person in law" was eventually banished.

As the 1860s dawned, the women's rights movement had been in existence for a dozen years. Activists had achieved progress on many fronts, but they saw few signs that the nation was seriously considering the enfranchisement of women. Most of the state petitions calling for women's suffrage in the 1850s met with little success. Then, in April 1861, the issue of slavery ignited a crisis that shook the United States to its core. When the Civil War began, most suffragists followed their abolitionist sentiments and supported the Union cause, while others embraced pacifism. But the more astute members of the movement realized that the war was going to bring about very big changes in the nation, and they hoped that those changes might bring women closer to equality.

Chapter Three
A QUESTION OF RIGHTS

―❦―

I do not see how anyone can pretend that there is the same urgency in giving the ballot to woman as to the negro. With us, the matter is a question of life and death.

—Frederick Douglass

NOW'S THE HOUR.—Not the "negro's hour" alone, but everybody's hour.

—Elizabeth Cady Stanton

At the outbreak of the Civil War in 1861, the women's rights movement came to a temporary standstill. Worried that the campaign would have trouble regaining its momentum, Susan B. Anthony opposed the idea of suspending suffrage operations, but she eventually bowed to the wishes of her colleagues. "All alike say, 'Have no convention at this crisis!,'" she wrote to a friend. "[William Lloyd] Garrison, [Wendell] Phillips, Mrs. Mott … Mrs. Stanton, etc. say, 'Wait until the war excitement abates.' I am sick at heart but I cannot carry the world against the wish and will of our best friends."

One positive effect of the war was that it provided new opportunities for women to show their mettle. Some women became directly involved in the war effort. Figures such as Clara Barton nursed soldiers on the battlefields, while a host of female volunteers helped organize medical care and other support for the Union Army through the United States Sanitary Commission. In addition, women took jobs in factories and offices and assumed control of family farms when men left their positions to serve in the military.

Though their activities slowed during the war, women's rights activists did not stop working completely. In 1863 Stanton, Anthony, Stone, and other leaders of the movement formed a new organization—the National Woman's Loyal League. The group's main focus was lobbying for the enactment of a new constitutional amendment to outlaw slavery throughout the United States. (President Lincoln had already issued the Emancipation Proclamation, but it abolished slavery only in the rebellious Southern states, not the entire nation.) Congress approved such an amendment—the Thirteenth—in early 1865, and it was ratified by the necessary three-quarters of the states ten months later, after the war had ended. Most people in the women's rights campaign strongly supported this measure. As it turned out, however, it was just one of several constitutional changes brought about by the war. The others proved much more divisive and triggered the most tumultuous period in the campaign for women's suffrage.

Expectations and Disappointment

Women's rights advocates initially felt great optimism during Reconstruction—the period immediately following the Civil War, when the country struggled to recover from the war's damages and reunite as a single nation. As one Northern proponent of female rights noted, women "did their full share in saving the Republic," and many anticipated that they would receive the right to vote as a reward for contributing to the Union victory. The activists also drew confidence from the fact that the Republican political party grew stronger after leading the successful war effort. Many women assumed that the party favored women's suffrage, because it included many of the progressive male politicians who had supported abolition and women's rights. Finally, the end of slavery in the United States had ushered in an era when democracy seemed to be on the rise. Suffragists expected to benefit from this expansion of political freedom.

Defining the exact limits of democracy proved to be a tricky process, however. While the Thirteenth Amendment had ended slavery, it had not given former slaves the right to vote. In fact, it had not even made them citizens of the United States. African Americans in the South still had no political power, which opened up the possibility that the same pro-slavery factions who had governed the South before the war might return to power. Many people feared that white Southerners would continue to exploit the powerless

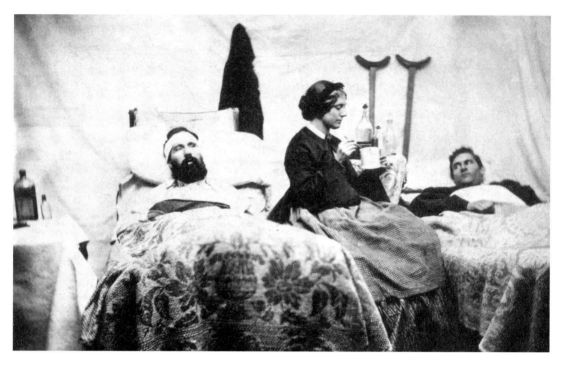

During the Civil War, women aided the war effort by serving as nurses and support staff for the U.S. Sanitary Commission.

black population—in effect creating a new kind of slavery. To avoid this situation, the Radical Republicans (members of the Republican party who favored a tough policy against the former Confederate states) introduced a draft version of a new constitutional amendment—the Fourteenth—in April 1866. The proposed amendment granted citizenship to African Americans and made it easier for them to vote in elections.

Suffragists hoped that the Fourteenth Amendment could be expanded to give the ballot to women as well, and they collected 10,000 signatures supporting this idea. But backers of the amendment refused to consider the notion. They knew that the enfranchisement of African Americans was controversial by itself; to add women into the mix would only increase the likelihood that the amendment would be voted down. In fact, the authors of the Fourteenth Amendment were careful to exclude women by specifically addressing the rights of "male inhabitants." This type of gender exclusion had not previously been part of the U.S. Constitution, and the leaders of the

31

The Lyceum

Following the Civil War, public lectures became an extremely popular form of entertainment throughout the United States—especially in the nation's small towns, where leisure activities were limited. A formal lecture circuit took shape, with companies booking speakers on extended tours. Generally known as the Lyceum, these lectures did not shy away from controversial subjects, such as women's rights—in fact, controversy helped fill seats. As a result, suffrage leaders became part of the circuit. Both Elizabeth Cady Stanton and Susan B. Anthony took part in the tours, and feminist advocate Anna E. Dickinson became a Lyceum superstar (see "Queen Anna" sidebar, p. 35).

The life of a Lyceum speaker could be a hard one. In an era when transportation was difficult, speakers chalked up thousands of miles of travel—with much of it taking place in the winter, when the audiences in farming towns had more free time available. Tallying a year's worth of touring in her diary, Anthony came up with a "full 13,000 miles travel—170 meetings." Stanton described the weariness and monotony of a two-month tour: "I must pack and unpack my trunk sixty-one times;... eat 183 more miserable meals;... shake hands with sixty-one more committees, smile, try to look intelligent and interested in everyone who approaches me, while I feel like a squeezed sponge."

The gains proved worth the difficulties, however. The Lyceum lectures spread the ideas of sexual equality to the far corners of the country, and the lucrative fees paid to the speakers were instrumental in keeping the suffrage leaders from sinking into bankruptcy. This combination delighted Stanton. "I have made $2,000 above all expenses since the middle of November," she wrote in 1870, "beside stirring up women generally to *rebellion*."

women's rights movement recognized that the language was dangerous. "If that word 'male' be inserted" in the Constitution, Stanton stated, "it will take us a century at least to get it out."

As the debate over the proposed Fourteenth Amendment intensified, many abolitionists who had once backed female suffrage either turned their backs on the issue or urged women to be patient. Wendell Phillips, a longtime proponent of women's rights, said that the nation should only address "one question at a time," and declared that "this hour belongs to the negro." In a meeting with Anthony and Stanton, Horace Greeley made a similar argument, telling the suffragists that "your turn will come next." In other words, women's suffrage would have to wait so that African American rights could be advanced.

The emphasis on securing African American rights was understandable given the decades of slavery and oppression they had endured prior to the Civil War—and troubling events in the postwar South. Racist groups such as the Ku Klux Klan had begun to terrorize blacks across the region. In May 1866 a group of former Confederate soldiers orchestrated a race riot in Memphis that left forty-six blacks dead and hundreds injured. In July of that year, violence in New Orleans killed thirty-four African Americans. Many activists believed that the best way to stem these attacks was to give blacks the vote as quickly as possible. They argued that African American voters would help elect progressive governments in the South that could take steps to stamp out violence. Black voters were also likely to favor Republican candidates—a fact that was well understood by the Republicans who promoted the new amendment.

In 1866, at the height of the controversy over the Fourteenth Amendment, women's rights supporters called a new convention. Attendees decided to form a new organization known as the American Equal Rights Association (AERA). This group included both women's rights advocates and members of the Anti-Slavery Society (many of the activists already belonged to both groups). The intent behind the AERA was to join the causes of woman's suffrage and African American suffrage, but this union proved difficult to achieve. Many members of the group favored passage of the Fourteenth Amendment as written. Figures such as Stanton and Anthony, on the other hand, felt reluctant to support an amendment that did not give the ballot to women.

Growing Hostility

In June 1866 both houses of Congress passed the Fourteenth Amendment and sent it to the states for ratification. The word "male" remained in the amendment, dealing a blow to women's rights. The ratification process stretched over two years. During that time, more and more of the suffragists' longtime allies deserted them. Newspaper publisher Horace Greeley, angry at Stanton and Anthony for their hard-nosed attempts to give women the vote

Horace Greeley, publisher of the *New York Tribune,* abandoned his support of women's rights during the battle over the Fourteenth Amendment.

in New York State, vowed that "no word of praise shall ever again be awarded you in the [New York] *Tribune.*" This withdrawal of support dealt the suffragists a serious blow, because Greeley's influential paper had been one of the few to support women's rights on a regular basis.

In 1867 the situation grew even more charged. The state of Kansas held a referendum in which voters were asked to consider two separate proposals: one giving the vote to women, and one giving the vote to African Americans. Most of the leaders of the women's rights movement traveled to Kansas to promote their cause, including Lucy Stone, Henry Blackwell, Elizabeth Cady Stanton, and Susan B. Anthony. Blackwell wrote that Kansas was "*the battle ground* for 1867. *It must not be allowed to fail.*" The foot soldiers received little support from their old allies in the Republican Party and the anti-slavery movement, however, and both measures were defeated. The suffragists felt betrayed. "Not one leading politician stood by us in the deadly breach," wrote Anthony. "They all mean to delude us into silence."

With their old support weakening, Stanton and Anthony began to seek new allies. In Kansas, Anthony appeared at rallies alongside George Francis Train, a wealthy and eccentric railroad financier who was a member of the Democratic Party. Train favored giving women the vote, but he was a vocal opponent of African American suffrage. In fact, his speeches were full of racist language, and on one occasion he clearly stated that "woman first, and Negro last is my programme." Other activists loathed Train. Lucy Stone considered him "a lunatic," while William Lloyd Garrison said that he was "mortified and astonished beyond measure in seeing Elizabeth Cady Stanton and Susan B. Anthony traveling about the country with that crackbrained harlequin."

But Stanton and Anthony dismissed such criticism and deepened their ties with the financier. The two women had been anxious to start their own

Queen Anna

Anna E. Dickinson

The public lecture circuit of the mid-1800s created celebrities whose status was similar to the radio, movie, and television stars of later decades. One of the biggest names of the 1860s was Anna E. Dickinson, an outspoken abolitionist and women's rights advocate.

Dickinson's appeal came partly from her youth (she began her speaking career in her late teens) and partly from her passionate and sometimes sarcastic speaking style. She made her breakthrough by campaigning on behalf of Republican candidates in 1863, and the following year she was invited to address President Lincoln and other dignitaries at the U.S. Capitol. After the Civil War, such standard speeches as "Woman's Work and Wages" and "Reconstruction" earned Dickinson as much as $1,000 per appearance and the nickname "Queen of the Lyceum."

Dickinson's fame proved fleeting, however. When her appeal as a speaker began to fade in the 1870s, she tried to start a new career as a playwright and actress but found little success. Illness and emotional problems took their toll, and she was committed to an insane asylum in the early 1890s. She eventually won her freedom in a court trial, but she spent the rest of her life out of the public eye.

newspaper, and Train agreed to bankroll the project. When *The Revolution* appeared in January 1868, it gave Stanton and Anthony a much-needed way to publicize their views, but it also featured inflammatory writings by Train that further weakened the equal-rights coalition. Anthony admitted Train's "idiosyncrasies," but claimed that she was willing to tolerate them because Train "is willing to devote energy and money to our cause when no other man is." Train's support proved fleeting, however. He soon left the country and ended up in a British prison for supporting Irish independence. *The Revolu-*

tion only survived for a little more than two years before it went bankrupt, leaving Anthony with $10,000 in debts.

In July 1868 the Fourteenth Amendment was ratified and became part of the U.S. Constitution. While the measure did enhance voting rights for African Americans, it did so in a roundabout way: it mandated punishment for states that prevented male citizens (including blacks) from voting, but it did not specifically prohibit states from denying a man's right to vote based on race. (The end result of this complicated plan was that Southern states received more severe punishment for denying the vote to blacks than did Northern states that engaged in the same practice.) Many proponents of African American rights thought the amendment was too weak, and they soon launched a campaign for a Fifteenth Amendment.

Compared with the Fourteenth Amendment, the wording of the proposed new amendment was simple and to the point: "The right of citizens of the United States to vote shall not be denied or abridged by the United States or by any State on account of race, color, or previous condition of servitude." But it started the debate about African American rights and women's rights all over again. Advocates of female suffrage wanted to insert the word "sex" into the amendment—which, if it passed, would have given females the right to vote. But once again, powerful figures argued that the need to secure African American rights was more pressing than the need to secure those of women. The debate over the Fifteenth Amendment provoked a crisis in the women's suffrage movement that had been looming for several years.

A Parting of the Ways

The more radical suffragists, led by Stanton and Anthony, decided to oppose the Fifteenth Amendment because it ignored women. They made this position clear in editorials that Stanton wrote for *The Revolution*. The more moderate activists, however, found that they could not abandon their ties to African American rights. They either supported the Fifteenth Amendment or refused to campaign against it. The moderates consisted mainly of the suffragists from New England, including Lucy Stone and Henry Blackwell. (The radical camp was now based in New York City, where Stanton had moved during the Civil War.)

When it became clear that Congress was going to pass the Fifteenth Amendment, the Stanton/Anthony faction immediately called for a new amendment—which would have been the Sixteenth—to give the vote to women. U.S. Representative George Julian introduced the draft version of this amendment in 1869. The measure stated that suffrage was to be based on citizenship, and that all citizens "shall enjoy this right equally without distinction or discrimination whatever founded on sex." The moderate suffragists were not necessarily opposed to a new amendment, but some urged a delay. They feared that the debate over a Sixteenth Amendment might slow the ratification process of the Fifteenth.

The proposed amendments were not the only issues that divided these groups. The moderates also felt uneasy about some of Stanton's views on marriage. For instance, she frequently advocated laws that would allow women to obtain a divorce more easily. While such laws became common in later decades, they were considered very radical in the 1860s. Stanton also made inflammatory statements about the institution of marriage, once describing it as "nothing more or less than legalized prostitution…. I rejoice over every slave that escapes from a discordant marriage."

Suffragists found an unlikely—and in many circles unwelcome—ally in the controversial railroad financier George Francis Train.

Anthony and Stanton's alliance with George Francis Train had also angered many of their progressive colleagues. This rift grew wider when Stanton began making negative comments about blacks and other minorities. In a January 1869 speech, for instance, she complained about "the lower orders of foreigners now crowding our shores" and used racial slurs to refer to blacks and Asians. (See "Elizabeth Cady Stanton Addresses the 1869 National Woman Suffrage Convention," p. 159) Through such speeches and her editorials in *The Revolution*, Stanton now argued for educated suffrage—claiming that the vote should only be given to those who had reached a certain level of education and familiarity with American traditions. This attitude made many suffragists uncomfortable. To them, Stanton's reasoning sounded very much like the argument that some whites in the South were then using to prohibit blacks from voting.

Abolition leader Frederick Douglass insisted that women's suffrage could wait until African American voting rights had been secured.

Matters came to a head at the American Equal Rights Association meeting in May 1869. (See "Divisions at the 1869 American Equal Rights Association Meeting," p. 164.) The discord started when Stephen Foster, a member of the moderate faction, chastised Stanton for her relationship with Train. Frederick Douglass spoke next. He began with words of praise for Stanton's support of equal rights, but then he voiced his displeasure with Stanton's recent opinions, especially her "employment of certain names such as 'Sambo' [a racial slur directed at African Americans]." Douglass went on to insist that African American suffrage was crucial and that women's needs were not as pressing. Many people in attendance were struck by the significance of this moment. Twenty years earlier in Seneca Falls, Douglass had stood beside Stanton and helped bring about the first call for women's suffrage. Now these old friends appeared to be parting ways.

The AERA members ignored Stanton and Anthony's protests against the Fifteenth Amendment and passed a resolution in support of the measure. Members of the moderate group also heaped more criticism upon Stanton, particularly regarding her views on marriage and divorce. The meeting adjourned with much bitterness on both sides. A few days later, Stanton and Anthony called together their supporters in New York. They agreed to form a separate organization, the National Woman's Suffrage Association (NWSA), with Stanton as its president. Members of the moderate faction were not invited to join the new group. Three months later, Lucy Stone began organizing a rival organization that would "unite those who cannot use the methods, and means, which Mrs. Stanton and Susan use." Stone's group called itself the American Woman Suffrage Association (AWSA).

With the formation of the NWSA and AWSA, the women's suffrage movement effectively tore itself in half. In March 1870 the Fifteenth Amendment became part of the U.S. Constitution, strengthening African American voting rights but leaving women disenfranchised. Meanwhile, the proposed Sixteenth Amendment giving women the right to vote became stalled in Congress and was never approved. The sense of promise that suffragists had felt at the close of the Civil War evaporated, and the activists entered a new decade with their hopes considerably dimmed.

Chapter Four

A MOVEMENT DIVIDED

⤜⧙⟊⧘⤛

We mean treason; we mean secession, and on a thousand times grander scale than was that of the South. We are plotting revolution; we will overslough this bogus republic and plant a government of righteousness in its stead, which shall not only profess to derive its power from the consent of the governed, but shall do so in reality.

—Victoria C. Woodhull, 1871

When the women's rights movement separated into two camps in 1869, the principal figures were forced to take sides. Stanton and Anthony's NWSA gathered a few prominent activists, including Ernestine Rose, Paulina Wright Davis, and Lucretia Mott—although Mott was in her early seventies and becoming less active (she would die in 1880). The majority of the high-profile activists joined Lucy Stone and Henry Blackwell in the AWSA. Among them were Antoinette Brown Blackwell, William Lloyd Garrison, Frances Gage, Frederick Douglass, Caroline Severance, Abby Kelly Foster, and the charismatic minister Henry Ward Beecher, who became the first president of the AWSA.

The presence of Beecher, Garrison, and Henry Blackwell illustrated one important difference between the two groups: the AWSA welcomed male members, while the NWSA was much more of a women's organization. At an early AWSA convention, Stone noted that "there have always been good and able men ready to second us, and to say their best words for our cause." On the other hand, an account of the formation of the NWSA in *History of Woman Suffrage* explained the founders' view that "there had been so much trouble

The Woman's Journal, published from 1870 to 1917, proved to be one of the most enduring voices in the campaign for women's suffrage.

with men in the Equal Rights Society, that it was thought best to keep the absolute control henceforth in the hands of women." In fact, Stanton had considered banning men from the NWSA altogether, but she was overruled. In 1870 the NWSA elected a man—progressive newspaper publisher Theodore Tilton—as its president. But Stanton and Anthony remained the group's true leaders, and they never overcame their distrust of the male reformers and politicians who, from their perspective, had let them down in the past.

Several other differences between the two sides soon emerged. The AWSA focused mostly on promoting state suffrage referendums and paid less attention to passing a national constitutional amendment. The NWSA, in contrast, took its cue from Stanton's 1869 call for a federal amendment. The organization therefore placed less emphasis on state measures, though it did not ignore state campaigns entirely.

The rival groups also sponsored competing publications. AWSA leaders Lucy Stone and Henry Blackwell founded the *Woman's Journal*, which went head-to-head against Stanton and Anthony's paper, *The Revolution*. Stone and Blackwell won this dual in short order, as *The Revolution* failed a few months after the first issue of the *Woman's Journal* appeared in January 1870. Graced by contributions from such notable writers as Harriet Beecher Stowe and Louisa May Alcott, the *Woman's Journal* would prove to be one of the most enduring voices in the campaign for women's suffrage. It continued publication until 1917, when it was succeeded by the *Woman Citizen*. The Blackwell family produced the *Journal* throughout that time, with Alice Stone Blackwell—the daughter of Lucy Stone and Henry Blackwell—taking over as its editor in 1893.

The biggest difference between the two organizations, however, could be found in their philosophies. The AWSA was the more conservative group. A resolution from the organization's semi-annual meeting in 1871 proclaimed its members' intention to "avoid side issues, and devote itself to the main question of suffrage." In other words, the AWSA did not concern itself with such matters as divorce law, contraception, or the role religion might play in the treatment of women. The NWSA, on the other hand, did not shy away from controversial issues. In fact, the group found itself embroiled in a major controversy in the early 1870s.

The Price of Free Love

In April 1870 a new figure emerged at the center of the women's rights movement: Victoria C. Woodhull (see biography on Woodhull, p. 144). Woodhull sent shock waves through the nation with the following words: "I announce myself as a candidate for the Presidency." The surprise candidate had almost no experience in politics or activism. Indeed, her past—once it was revealed—included such dubious pursuits as peddling bottled elixirs and working as a spiritual clairvoyant. But Woodhull was more than a sideshow hustler. With the help of millionaire Cornelius Vanderbilt, she had become a wealthy investment banker, and she was consumed with the mission of improving women's lives. Though she had no real chance of becoming president of United States in the 1872 election, her campaign created a great deal of publicity—both for herself and for the women's rights movement as a whole. (This tactic would be repeated by another woman—Belva Lockwood—in 1880 and 1884.)

Shortly after announcing her candidacy, Woodhull became involved in another incident that attracted more publicity. In a January 1871 address before the judiciary committees of both houses of Congress, she made a startling declaration: women already had the right to vote. Woodhull presented a detailed argument concerning the Fourteenth and Fifteenth Amendments to the Constitution. She claimed that these amendments had guaranteed that women were citizens, and had also guaranteed all citizens—"all people of both sexes"—the right to vote. Woodhull was not the first person to make this argument, but she was the only person who got the chance to make it before Congress. Although her views were later dismissed by the congressional committees—and ultimately denied by the Supreme Court—the address injected a jolt of energy into the women's suffrage movement.

WASHINGTON, D. C.—THE JUDICIARY COMMITTEE OF THE HOUSE OF REPRESENTATIVES RECEIVING A DEPUTATION OF FEMALE SUFFRAGISTS, JANUARY 11TH.—A LADY DELEGATE READING HER ARGUMENT IN FAVOR OF WOMAN'S VOTING, ON THE BASIS OF THE FOURTEENTH AND FIFTEENTH CONSTITUTIONAL AMENDMENTS.—SEE PAGE 347.

In a historic 1871 address before Congress, Victoria C. Woodhull argued that existing Constitutional amendments already guaranteed women the right to vote.

Many historians question whether Woodhull actually wrote the historic address. Most believe that the real author was Senator Benjamin Butler, a friend and supporter of Woodhull who had arranged for her appearance at the Capitol. In any case, Woodhull made an impression with her personal charisma. The NWSA soon embraced her, and she spoke at two of the association's meetings in 1871 (See "The Great Secession Speech of Victoria C. Woodhull," p. 169). Elizabeth Cady Stanton called her "a grand, brave woman," and Susan B. Anthony told Woodhull that she had "inspired the strongest of us with new hope and enthusiasm."

Other suffragists, however, found Woodhull considerably less impressive—particularly the members of the more conservative AWSA. In fact, they found some of the presidential candidate's controversial ideas to be alarming. Most controversial of all was Woodhull's support for the concept of "free love." (This was the nineteenth-century term for sexual liberation, or the belief that romantic relationships did not require the sanction of marriage.)

This view directly contradicted the conventional idea that men and women were meant to be joined in a permanent, religiously sanctioned union. Those who believed in free love argued that love was the key factor in achieving happiness—not the legal and religious bond. Going further, some argued that traditional marriage was a destructive force in society, because it trapped women in a permanent arrangement where they had little power and thus could be exploited by their husbands. Most advocates of free love denied that they were in favor of loose morals and promiscuity, but that remained the popular perception. Critics in the press often labeled their intentions as "free lust" rather than free love.

Marriage had been a sensitive topic for the suffragists for many years. One of the sharpest criticisms of the women's rights movement was that its demands would eventually destroy families. The more conservative suffragists thus tried to avoid any policies that appeared to weaken the family structure. For instance, they objected to Elizabeth Cady Stanton's promotion of more liberal divorce laws. Victoria Woodhull was far more radical than Stanton—or at least more willing to state her views openly. "*I am a free lover!*," she proclaimed in an 1871 speech. "I have an inalienable, constitutional, and natural right to love whom I may, to love for as long or as short a period as I can, to change that love everyday if I please!" Such statements made Woodhull a media sensation, and before long newspapers began to associate the entire women's rights movement with the idea of free love.

In light of the negative publicity Woodhull brought to the movement, Anthony began to have second thoughts about supporting her campaign. Stanton, on the other hand, remained a firm supporter of Woodhull. This difference of opinion led to a bitter dispute between the two women in 1872, when Stanton wanted to link the NWSA to Woodhull's Equal Rights Party. Anthony refused to go along with this plan, and she also refused to allow Woodhull on the stage at the NWSA convention. When the candidate's supporters threatened to take over the proceedings, Anthony ordered the janitor to shut off the gaslights in the hall, preventing Woodhull from addressing the delegates.

Anthony's reservations proved wise. In the months before the election, Woodhull's campaign faltered, beset by financial woes and public scorn for her unconventional views. But before her presidential campaign collapsed completely, Woodhull seized the spotlight one final time. On several previous occasions, Woodhull had threatened to reveal scandalous information about

Empowered by the Spirits

Among her other controversial activities, Victoria Woodhull was an avowed spiritualist who claimed to communicate with the dead. Belief in supernatural forces was not uncommon in the mid-1800s, nor was Woodhull the only member of the suffrage movement to be involved with such beliefs. In fact, the table on which the movement's pioneers drafted the Declaration of Sentiments for the Seneca Falls Convention was known as a "spirit table" because its owners, Thomas and Mary Ann McClintock, believed that it helped conduct thoughts to and from those who had passed into the afterlife.

In her book *Other Powers: The Age of Suffrage, Spiritualism, and the Scandalous Victoria Woodhull*, Barbara Goldsmith writes that "it was to women that the appeal of Spiritualism was especially potent." In an age when large numbers of children died from disease, seances gave mothers a chance to reconnect with their lost sons and daughters. Goldsmith also suggests that women called upon the spirits to provide "words of comfort, reassurance, and power that women, even the strongest, so desperately needed." This certainly seemed to be true of Woodhull, who once attributed her commanding stage presence to unseen forces. "As I am about to speak, I call upon the spirits," she noted. "They surround me and protect me. I sense them hovering about me in the air ... and the light beaming through. I am doing their bidding."

influential figures unless they supported her run for office. She finally carried through on her threat in November 1872.

Woodhull's paper—*Woodhull and Claflin's Weekly*—published a story charging that Henry Ward Beecher, an influential minister and the former president of the AWSA, had carried on an adulterous affair. Even more scandalous, the story revealed that Beecher's lover was Elizabeth Tilton, the wife of publisher Theodore Tilton, who had served as president of the NWSA. Many people within the suffrage movement already knew of the affair, but Woodhull announced the racy details to the world. As a result of the story—and other sexually charged stories in the same issue—she and her sister (co-publisher of the paper) were arrested for sending obscenity through the mail. They spent seven months in jail, but they were eventually found not guilty.

In publishing the sensational story, Woodhull had intended to show that people like Beecher were hypocrites because they practiced free love at the same time that they condemned it. But the resulting controversy caused great harm to the women's rights movement. It created the perception that suffragists were sinful radicals, which alienated many potential supporters. "There was never such a foolish muddle," Anthony observed. "Our movement ... is so demoralized by the letting go of the helm of the ship to Woodhull."

The influential minister Henry Ward Beecher, who played an active role in both the abolition and suffrage movements.

Wins in the West

As the national women's suffrage organizations dealt with scandal, discord, and disappointment, some promising developments occurred on the western frontier. In 1869 Wyoming Territory became the first area in the country to give women the unrestricted right to vote. Perhaps because Wyoming was not yet a state, this victory received relatively little notice from the national organizations, but it served as an important precedent. In the coming decades, almost all of the suffrage victories took place in western territories and states. Historians have cited several factors to account for this development. Some point to the challenges of frontier living, which often forced men and women to work closely together to establish farms and communities. As a result, men in the west became accustomed to viewing women as equals. In addition, the people who found their way to the frontier tended to be independent-minded mavericks, go-for-broke risk-takers, or desperate individuals with few other choices. None of them felt a strong need to do things in a traditional manner.

In 1870 the Utah Territory became the second locale to enfranchise women. Once again, the national suffrage organizations provided no input. (In fact, the AWSA and NWSA avoided Utah because they did not want to be associated with the Mormons, some of whom practiced polygamy.) In *A History of the American Suffrage Movement*, historian Doris Weatherford argues that the lack of involvement by national figures may have been a blessing in some of the western states, because the residents seemed to resent the interference of outsiders. There had been some evidence of such a backlash during the unsuccessful Kansas campaign of 1867, when suffrage leaders from the eastern United States had done a great deal of campaigning.

As it turned out, though, a number of female settlers in the west proved willing to shoulder the burden themselves. Activist Jessie Haver Butler remembered her mother conducting her own personal campaign for the vote during the successful push for women's suffrage in Colorado in the early 1890s. "My father had a highly organized dairy with hired men whom she had to feed, as well as her children. Yet, I remember vividly … how she climbed into that spring wagon," Butler related. "She toured that valley to get the men to vote for woman's suffrage. And this wasn't something that a good little housewife, even in Colorado, in those days was supposed to do." One of the most prominent western suffragists was Abigail Scott Duniway, who had traveled to Oregon on a pioneer wagon train in the 1850s and later championed women's rights throughout the Pacific Northwest (see biography on Duniway, p. 116).

Testing the Laws

While suffragists worked to pass new laws and amendments granting women the right to vote, they also attacked the issue on another front—by challenging the legality of the existing laws that barred them from voting. Victoria Woodhull's 1871 address before Congress was one such effort, but there were many others. In several different incidents in the late 1860s and early 1870s, women attempted to cast votes in elections. These activists hoped to be arrested for illegal voting so that they could pursue their legal case all the way to the Supreme Court. They believed that the justices might rule, as Woodhull had argued, that the provisions of the Fourteenth and Fifteenth Amendments had enfranchised women.

These direct actions reached a peak during the presidential election of 1872. The most celebrated incident took place in Rochester, New York, where Susan B. Anthony had managed to register a group of women voters prior to the election. On the day of the election, Anthony expected that she and her

During the late 1800s, many women tested the laws that prohibited them from voting.

followers would be denied the right to cast their ballots, which would give them the chance to file a lawsuit. To their surprise, however, they were allowed to vote. "Well I have been & gone & done it!!," Anthony wrote to Stanton. "Positively voted the Republican ticket.... We are in for a fine agitation in Rochester." Several weeks later Anthony and the other women were arrested for illegal voting. Although Anthony did not succeed in getting her case before the Supreme Court, she used her trial to make an impassioned protest against the legal status of women (see "Susan B. Anthony Reacts to Her Conviction for Unlawful Voting," p. 172).

The suffragists finally did receive a hearing before the Supreme Court, but it did not provide the result they desired. The case involved Virginia Minor, president of the Missouri Woman Suffrage Association. She and her husband brought a lawsuit against election inspectors after she was prevented from voting in 1872. The case made its way to the Supreme Court, which ruled against the Minors on March 29, 1875. The ruling specified that voting was a matter to be regulated by the states. Therefore, the justices argued, the United States Constitution did not give anyone the right to vote; it could only prevent certain forms of discrimination in voting. Since the Fourteenth and Fifteenth Amendments prohibited discrimination on the basis of race rather than sex, women did not have the right to vote. The ruling provided yet another source of disappointment for the suffragists, but it did help clarify their mission. They now knew that their only hopes involved changing the voting laws in individual states or pursuing a federal constitutional amendment that would prohibit discrimination based on sex.

Progress continued on both fronts. Suffragists succeeded in bringing the issue before voters in six states in the 1870s and 1880s (four of them west of the Mississippi River), but in each of these elections the suffrage measure went down in defeat. In 1883 the legislature of Washington Territory gave women the vote, but the Supreme Court struck down the measure four years later. A similar development occurred in Utah: as part of the ongoing struggle over polygamy, the U.S. Congress passed a bill that rescinded women's right to vote in the territory. Although Montana Territory gave women the vote in 1887, the loss of female voting rights in Washington and Utah meant that the local suffrage campaigns actually lost ground in the 1880s.

Still, some activists took heart from the fact that a large number of so-called partial suffrage measures were enacted during this period. These laws allowed women to vote on certain issues, such as education or alcohol

This National Woman's Suffrage Association meeting took place in 1880—during the period when the movement was split into two opposing factions.

reform. By 1890 nineteen states had enacted some form of partial suffrage. However, the more ardent reformers disliked these "half" measures. They pointed out that partial suffrage still left women with fewer rights than men. Critics also claimed that politicians used these bills to pay lip service to women's rights without enacting any truly meaningful legislative changes.

The news was not much better at the federal level. The constitutional amendment that had been introduced in 1869 had gone nowhere. In 1878 Senator Arlen A. Sargeant of California introduced a new draft amendment which stated that "the right of citizens of the United States to vote shall not be denied or abridged by the United States or by any State on account of sex." This was the same amendment that would finally give women the vote, but its passage was still more than forty years in the future. (It was originally known as the Sixteenth Amendment, but as the years passed and other amendments came up for consideration, it was dubbed the Susan B. Anthony Amendment.)

Though the amendment was reintroduced in each session of Congress, it was almost never brought to the floor of the House or Senate for a vote. When a vote did take place in the Senate in 1887, the measure lost by a wide margin.

Clearly, suffragists had a lot of work to do. But the movement was still divided between two national organizations that often worked at cross-purposes. Some of the younger activists began to urge a reunion between the AWSA and NWSA. Harriot Stanton Blatch (daughter of Elizabeth Cady Stanton) and Alice Stone Blackwell (daughter of Lucy Stone and Henry Blackwell) proved especially active in this regard. As the final decade of the 1800s loomed, they provided hope that the two-decade rift in the women's suffrage movement might finally be mended.

Chapter Five

A CHANGING OF THE GUARD

⬥

Lucy [Stone] and Susan [B. Anthony] alike see suffrage only....
They do not see women's religious and social bondage. Neither do the young women in either association, hence they
may as well combine for they have one mind and purpose.

—Elizabeth Cady Stanton

In 1890 the rival AWSA and NWSA agreed to merge into a single group, to be known as the National American Woman Suffrage Association (NAWSA). Several factors contributed to the merger. First and foremost, the groups were no longer as far apart in philosophy as they had once been. Beginning with the Victoria Woodhull incident, Anthony had helped steer the NWSA away from such controversial side issues as religion and marriage. As a result, its mission became more focused on suffrage, like that of the AWSA.

Deciding on a leader for the new organization proved surprisingly pain-less. Stone refused to be considered for the presidency due to ill health—she would die just three years later. Both Anthony and Stanton received nomina-tions for the top post, but once again Anthony yielded the spotlight to her friend. Stanton's presidency turned out to be more honorary than active, which was little surprise. Her involvement in the suffrage movement had been inconsistent since the late 1860s. At times she took a large role in NWSA affairs, but she also withdrew for extended periods, leaving Anthony to handle operation of the group on her own. Anthony had complained about Stanton's lack of involvement in 1871, telling her friend that "there was never such a suicidal letting go as has been yours these last two years.... How you can excuse yourself is more than I can understand." In the 1880s Stanton quit

The long working relationship between suffrage pioneers Elizabeth Cady Stanton (seated) and Susan B. Anthony became strained in the late 1800s.

her lecture tours and began spending a lot of time in England and France, where her children lived.

In the meantime, Anthony's commitment to the movement never wavered. Though she initially held the title of vice president at large in NAWSA, she was much more active than Stanton, and in 1892 she became the group's president. Even at the age of seventy-four, Anthony continued to travel across the country promoting suffrage. In 1893 she visited Colorado, which held a referendum on women's voting rights that year. The measure passed, giving the suffrage movement its first major victory in ten years. Colorado activist Jessie Haver Butler later recalled that Anthony was "all over the state…. She walked, she rode donkeys." Since many of the state's small mining towns lacked public meeting space, Anthony often made speeches in saloons—which was no small concession for the lifelong foe of alcohol. "She was a sensation," remembered Butler. "Susan B. Anthony was such a sweet and gracious person. That she would take the trouble to go into the saloon and talk to the men, that's one way that Colorado got the vote."

Another key to the Colorado victory was Carrie Chapman Catt, a representative of the new generation of suffrage leaders. Catt had lived for many years in Iowa, so she had a better rapport with the western voters than many of the suffragists from the eastern United States. She also adopted a new approach toward alcohol, an issue that had contributed to many of the election losses in other states.

Since its earliest days, the women's suffrage movement had forged a close relationship with temperance reformers. By the 1880s, in fact, Susan B.

Anthony and others had collaborated with the powerful National Women's Christian Temperance Union (see sidebar "God, Voting, and Frances Willard," p. 62). The relationship between the two organizations, though, contributed to a widespread belief that women would promote anti-alcohol legislation if they won the vote. This scenario alarmed brewers, distillers, and saloon owners, and these groups contributed large amounts of money to defeat women's suffrage in state elections.

In Colorado, however, Catt worked hard to downplay the issue of temperance. Her strategy helped overcome voter opposition to the suffrage measure. She employed the same tactic three years later in Idaho and scored a second victory. Catt also played an important role in reorganizing NAWSA in the mid-1890s. She urged the group to create new committees to coordinate nationwide activities and pursue fundraising.

Organized Opposition to Suffrage

Around the same time that NAWSA leaders improved their organization, the suffragists also found themselves facing more organized opposition. The first anti-suffrage group had been formed in 1869, and several formal and informal opposition groups—collectively known as "antis"—had emerged in the succeeding decades. But the anti-suffrage movement really took off in the mid-1890s.

The antis used some of the same tactics that the suffragists utilized: sponsoring petition drives, visiting legislators, making public speeches, and publishing pamphlets and newspaper articles. They promoted the same ideas that had been voiced by previous opponents of suffrage. Antis frequently stated that a woman's proper role was as a mother and keeper of the home, for example; they claimed that voting would serve to destroy the distinctions between the sexes, erode traditional family structures, and cast society into upheaval. But they also tossed a range of other objections into the mix, variously claiming that only people who could serve in the military should be allowed to vote; that the enfranchisement of women would encourage only disreputable females to vote; that women had not bothered to vote in those places where they already had the ballot; and that even when women did participate, their votes had little effect on the outcome of elections. As with most forms of propaganda, the truthfulness of these claims was less important than the fact that they got people's attention.

Anti-suffrage forces claimed that granting women the right to vote would harm the traditional family structure. In this cartoon, an angry man returns home from work to find that his wife left the children alone to attend a suffrage meeting.

Perhaps the most potent argument put forth by the antis was that most American women simply did not want the right to vote. "We believe the great majority of women in this country are either against woman suffrage or entirely indifferent to it," stated an article in the anti-suffrage publication *Woman's Protest*. To support this position, the antis pointed out that most attempts to give women the vote at the turn of the twentieth century had failed. One anti-suffrage writer noted that between 1898 and 1909 "not one single pro-suffrage law has been passed in this country."

The fact that most of the anti-suffrage activists were women lent credence to their claims. If these women actively opposed suffrage, the thinking went, there must be many more women who felt the same way. NAWSA and other suffrage groups tended to dismiss the antis or accuse them of being fronts for the liquor industry—a charge that was widely discussed but never really proven. In any case, the antis proved to be stubborn foes with significant staying power. In 1911 the antis formed a nationwide organization, the National Association Opposed to Woman Suffrage. By 1916 it claimed 350,000 members.

Suffrage and Race

The common perception of the suffragists was that they were white women from the middle- or upper-middle classes. That characterization may have been true of the majority of members in the national organizations, but in reality the movement included many diverse groups. African American

The Women's Club Movement

Women may have had a difficult time securing voting rights in the decades following the Civil War, but their interest and involvement in issues outside the home increased steadily during this period. Unable to attend college without negotiating a host of daunting societal and financial hurdles, women eager to educate themselves began forming clubs in which they could study such subjects as history and literature. As the number of working women increased, professional organizations for females also formed, with the Sorosis Club being the best known. African American women formed clubs as well, with the National Association of Colored Women (NACW) becoming the largest group.

Many of these groups chose to focus on community issues, and by the 1890s many of them had taken up Progressive social issues like poverty, prison conditions, and alcohol abuse. In addition, after seeing how voting rights could benefit their social work, many club members became suffragists. The clubs sometimes formally endorsed votes for women. The NACW, for example, took this step upon its founding in 1896. Other groups were more hesitant to link themselves to women's voting rights, but in time many took that step. The General Federation of Women's Clubs, an umbrella group for white clubs, formally endorsed suffrage in 1914.

leaders like Frederick Douglass and Sojourner Truth had pursued the vote for women since the earliest days of the movement. This source of support grew stronger in the late 1800s thanks to the spread of African American women's clubs (see sidebar "The Women's Club Movement").

Many of these clubs expressed their eagerness to aid the national suffrage organization, but NAWSA gave them the cold shoulder. In 1894, for example, a group of black activists approached Susan B. Anthony about gaining membership in NAWSA. Anthony refused their request, worried that the presence of blacks would alienate potential supporters. These discriminatory actions on the part of the suffrage leaders angered African American activists such as Ida B. Wells-Barnett (see biography on Wells-Barnett, p. 136). "Although [Anthony] may have made gains for suffrage," Wells-Barnett said,

Mary Church Terrell, leader of the National Association of Colored Women (NACW), advocated voting rights for African American women.

"she had also confirmed white women in their attitude of segregation." NAWSA continued to discourage participation by African Americans well into the 1900s, though a small number of black members joined integrated local chapters of the association.

The rejection by NAWSA did not stop black women from pursuing the vote. In 1896 two smaller groups combined to form the National Association of Colored Women (NACW). Headed by Mary Church Terrell, this organization pushed for female voting rights from its earliest days and boasted some 400 chapters by 1900. The Women's Convention, a part of the National Baptist Convention, also mobilized blacks in support of female voting rights.

While the national suffrage organizations increasingly shunned blacks, membership grew among whites in the South. Support for women's rights had generally been weak in the former Confederate states, partly due to the historic association between the women's movement and the abolition movement. More Southern whites had warmed to idea of women voters by the late 1800s, but in some cases that support was linked to notions of racial superiority. Ever since the Reconstruction era, the issue of African American voting rights in the former slave states had been a divisive one. Some whites who wished to prevent blacks from gaining political power advanced the idea of enfranchising women as a means of balancing the votes cast by black men. Of course, the effect of white women's votes would be limited if black women got the vote at the same time. Therefore, proponents of this type of plan usually urged that only educated women be allowed to vote (see "Belle Kearney Discusses Women's Suffrage in the South," p. 181). With fewer opportunities for schooling, many black women would fail to meet the education standards, thus giving whites an electoral advantage.

Such arguments were not new. In fact, Stanton and Anthony had advanced the idea of educated suffrage as early as the 1860s. But in the 1890s black men were systematically denied the right to vote throughout the South through the imposition of poll taxes, literacy tests, and other requirements. Liberal suffragists opposed such restrictions, and they also viewed the educated suffrage plans as racist in nature. The rhetoric employed by the Southern suffragists often revealed the true intentions behind these plans.

Despite such liberal opposition, however, suffrage chapters from the South (those with a white membership, that is) remained welcome in the national organization. In 1903 the NAWSA executive committee even vowed that "the doctrine of States' rights is recognized in the national body" and that "each auxiliary State association arranges its own affairs in accordance with its own ideas." In other words, NAWSA leaders allowed the state chapters in the South to pursue whatever methods they wished regarding educated suffrage. In this way NAWSA failed to take a strong stand against Southern discrimination. Coupled with the organization's refusal to accept black chapters, these developments made it clear that national suffrage leaders hoped to avoid controversy by adopting a conservative stance on race relations.

The End of an Era

NAWSA's final interaction with Elizabeth Cady Stanton provided yet another sign of the association's growing conservatism. Though she had always professed more radical views than most of her fellow suffragists, Stanton saved her most controversial arguments for the final decade of her life. In 1895 she published the first volume of *The Woman's Bible*, which analyzed the Old and New Testaments and presented evidence to dispute the commonly held notion that the Bible sanctioned the inferior status of women. The book created an uproar among religious leaders, who called it blasphemous and the work of the devil.

Responding to this criticism, NAWSA members adopted a resolution at their January 1896 convention declaring that the association "has no official connection with the so-called *Woman's Bible*." This resolution was a sharp rebuke to the woman who had co-founded the organization and helped launch the campaign for women's suffrage. Stanton urged Anthony to resign her presidency in protest, but Anthony declined, claiming that she wanted to stay on to "try to reverse this miserable narrow action."

In reality, however, Anthony bore a great deal of responsibility for NAWSA's "narrowness." She had moved the group away from its more radical

Carrie Chapman Catt played an important role in reversing the fortunes of the women's suffrage movement around the turn of the twentieth century.

views in hopes of securing suffrage. In her mind, gaining the vote had become the all-important first step in women's liberation. "You say 'women must be emancipated from their superstitions before enfranchisement will be of any benefit,'" she wrote in a letter to Stanton, "and I say just the reverse, that women must be enfranchised before they can be emancipated from their superstitions."

Anthony continued to serve as president of NAWSA for four more years, finally stepping down in 1900, at the age of eighty. She chose Carrie Chapman Catt as her successor, calling Catt "my ideal leader." Catt's first tenure as president was a short one, however. She resigned in 1904 to care for her ill husband, though she would return to the group and become an important player in the 1910s. Upon Catt's departure, the Reverend Anna Howard Shaw became president.

With the deaths of Elizabeth Cady Stanton in 1902 and Susan B. Anthony in 1906, the first phase of the suffrage campaign came to an end. Their passing left the movement in the hands of people who knew the pre-Civil War era as history rather than as personal experience. Stanton and Anthony's deaths also reinforced the fact that women had been fighting for the vote for more than fifty years. During that time they had only succeeded in four western states: Wyoming, Colorado, Idaho, and Utah—the last having reinstated woman's suffrage in 1896.

Taking Stock of the Suffrage Cause

This lack of progress led some activists to question the methods that had been used in the past. They took a hard look at the National American Woman Suffrage Association and found that the group faced two glaring problems as it entered the twentieth century: it had few members and little money. According to historian Sara Hunter Graham in *Woman Suffrage and the New Democracy*, NAWSA had about 8,900 dues-paying members in 1900 and an equal number that did not contribute. This total compared unfavorably to many national organizations. For instance, the Women's Christian Temperance Union, one of the largest women's groups of the era, boasted hundreds of thousands of members.

NAWSA experienced financial difficulties due to its low membership and contribution figures. Some chapters contributed less than $10 per year to the national treasury. As a result, NAWSA was unable to afford the increasingly sophisticated methods of political promotion and public relations that were then becoming common. For instance, NAWSA had no permanent staff in Washington, D.C., to lobby Congress on behalf of the Susan B. Anthony Amendment. The lack of personnel and money also contributed to a lack of initiative. Although Susan B. Anthony's final speech to NAWSA had featured the rousing statement "failure is impossible," Carrie Chapman Catt expressed a more sober opinion of the group's chance for success. In 1898 Catt suggested that "the hopeless, lifeless, faithless members of our own organization" presented the greatest obstacle to NAWSA's goals. "'It cannot be done' is their favorite motto," she lamented.

Upon taking over the presidency of NAWSA, Catt took action to remedy these shortcomings. Anna Howard Shaw continued this work when the organization came under her leadership. The thrust of their plan involved converting more of the country's affluent women to the cause of suffrage. To a certain extent, the woman's rights movement had always been pursued more actively by the middle and upper classes than by the poor. Financially secure women had more free time available to devote to social causes, and they also tended to have greater exposure to progressive ideas.

Catt and Shaw, aided by Kentucky suffragist Laura Clay (see biography on Clay, p. 113), sought to expand NAWSA's membership among the wealthy elite, a group that had not previously been involved in the movement. They reached out to women's clubs and also employed a new tool called the "parlor meeting." These gatherings took place in private homes and usually included a small group of women. They proved attractive to people who did not feel comfortable attending a larger public meeting on a somewhat controversial subject. "You had these little afternoon gatherings of women, maybe six or eight women," remembered Sylvie Thygeson, an organizer in St. Paul, Minnesota. "While we were drinking tea, I gave them a little talk.... It was a very nice, interesting social time for meeting people and enjoying ourselves."

God, Voting, and Frances Willard

Frances E. Willard

From its beginning, the women's suffrage movement was entwined with the fight against alcohol consumption. No figure better represented the mingling of the two causes than Frances E. Willard, president of Women's Christian Temperance Union (WCTU). After taking charge of the organization in 1881, Willard built the WCTU into the most powerful women's group in the country.

An ardent suffragist, Willard once claimed that God had instructed her to "speak for woman's ballot as a weapon of protection …from the tyranny of drink." While local WCTU chapters were allowed to decide their own positions with regard to female voting rights, Willard's views undoubtedly brought many new converts to the suffrage cause. This delighted Susan B. Anthony, who had been a temperance reformer before she joined the suffrage movement.

More liberal suffragists, however, were not always comfortable with Willard's strict religious views. Elizabeth Cady Stanton spoke out against Willard's efforts to make Christianity the official religion of the United States. Matilda Joslyn Gage, who shared Stanton's views on religion, called Willard "the most dangerous person on the American continent today." But even Willard's enemies had to admire her skill and energy. Prior to her death in 1898, she did her best to fulfill her motto of "do everything," making the WCTU a factor in issues ranging from child care to prison reform to prostitution.

The new, wealthy recruits had the means to contribute generously to the cause, which helped solve NAWSA's financial problems. By 1916, the association had an operating budget of $100,000 per year. The upper-class women also made suffrage seem more fashionable, which helped attract more women from all walks of life. As a result, the association's membership increased to 117,000 by 1910.

Another factor working in the suffragists' favor was that their efforts took place at the height of the Progressive Era. During this period, reformers publicized a range of social problems, including political corruption, unsafe work conditions, and overcrowded slums. It was a time when activism became more widely accepted throughout America and new ideas enjoyed lively discussion. But discussing suffrage was not necessarily the same thing as making it happen. While NAWSA had more members and more money by the end of the first decade of the 1900s, the movement had not made any concrete gains. No states had been added to the suffrage column, and little progress had been made toward passage of the federal amendment. Chafing at the lack of tangible progress, some suffragists started to contemplate new approaches to winning the vote.

Chapter Six

CONSERVATIVES AND RADICALS

·······

The essence of the campaign ... is opposition to the government.

—Alice Paul

As the level of disenchantment increased among NAWSA members, so did criticism of the suffrage organization's president, Anna Howard Shaw. Shaw was famous for her oratorical skills, but critics began to feel she was more interested in making speeches to the membership and staging pageant-filled conventions than in formulating a viable plan for winning the vote. Most of the innovative ideas that emerged between 1905 and 1916 came from outside the NAWSA leadership. In many cases these plans were initiated by activists who had grown frustrated with the inability of the president and her closest advisors to advance the suffrage cause.

One of the new ideas involved bringing the message of suffrage to the working class—particularly to working-class women. Organizers of the movement had largely ignored this group throughout the 1800s—with one notable exception. In the late 1860s Susan B. Anthony had helped form the Workingwoman's Association in New York City, which lent support to women engaged in such work as typesetting and sewing. As part of this effort, Anthony tried to form an alliance with the National Labor Union, but the relationship ran into problems and did not last long. From that point on, the suffrage movement distanced itself from labor groups and kept its focus on the more affluent levels of society. This was especially true in the late 1800s, when Anthony, Lucy Stone, and other suffrage leaders

Anna Howard Shaw drew criticism from fellow suffragists during her tenure as president of NAWSA.

made winning the vote their central aim and ignored such issues as women's pay and workplace conditions. In addition, racial and ethnic bigotry and language barriers made it difficult for the white middle-class activists to reach out to those workers who had immigrated to the United States from southern and central Europe.

Several suffragists worked to bridge this divide in the early 1900s. One example is Jane Addams, a well-known social reformer who had founded Hull House in Chicago—a "settlement house" that offered classes, child care, and other services to poor immigrants. Addams strongly supported women's suffrage, and her rapport with working women and immigrants helped to spread the message among these groups. She also published essays that explained why women deserved the vote and how working-class women could use it to improve their lives.

Harriot Stanton Blatch, the daughter of Elizabeth Cady Stanton, also helped attract working-class women to the suffrage movement. Blatch returned to the United States in the early 1900s after living in England for twenty years. Britain experienced its own women's suffrage movement during this period, and activists there made a concerted appeal to the working class. Blatch decided to adapt the English tactic to the United States. She formed the Equality League of Self-Supporting Women in 1907, which actively promoted female voting rights among working women.

These sorts of efforts had the potential to reach a lot of people. According to Alexander Keyssar in *The Right to Vote*, women made up one-fifth of the American work force in 1900. In New York City, where Blatch based her efforts, 50,000 women worked in the garment industry alone. The Equality League proved innovative in its organizing tactics, holding large outdoor rallies and also staging the nation's first suffrage parade. The group's membership climbed to 20,000 in the space of a decade.

Grassroots Victories

In 1910 the suffragists broke their long drought and began winning state referenda that gave women the vote. As before, the victories came in western states, and in most cases they resulted from local campaigns that had little to do with the national organization. In fact, many of the western activists turned down assistance from NAWSA's main office, feeling that it would be more harmful than helpful. Some of this antagonism grew out of events in Oregon in 1906, when NAWSA had taken a large role in the campaign for a suffrage referendum only to see it fail.

Second-generation activist Harriot Stanton Blatch voices her disapproval during a 1915 anti-suffrage rally.

The first suffrage battle of the 1910s took place in Washington State, where women had been allowed to vote for four years during the territorial period. In order to get the referendum on the ballot, suffragists needed the support of state legislators. They gained this support through lobbying efforts that were both traditional and innovative. One of the new approaches involved sending young, attractive women to visit male politicians, with instructions to remain pleasant and "never bore a legislator by too much insistence." Newspaper reporters described these visitors as "a constant wonder to the legislators …[who] had expected another type [of woman and] arguments."

Once they succeeded in placing the measure on the ballot, state organizers formed coalitions with other progressive groups—such as labor unions and farmers-rights organizations—and kept the issue of prohibition in the background. The measure passed by a wide margin, making Washington the first state to approve women's suffrage in the twentieth century. The following year California gave women the vote. During that campaign, activists repeated some of the tactics used in Washington and also pioneered new techniques, such as billboard advertising.

After California, suffragists registered a succession of other triumphs at the state level: Arizona, Kansas, and Oregon approved women's suffrage in

Alice Paul introduced radical protest methods to the campaign for women's suffrage.

1912; Montana and Nevada followed suit in 1914; New York became the first eastern state to adopt the measure in 1917; and Michigan, Oklahoma, and South Dakota granted women the vote in 1918. Women in fifteen states enjoyed the right to vote by the end of the 1910s.

These victories proved immensely important in the eventual passage of the Nineteenth Amendment. First, they demonstrated a definite trend toward enfranchising women. Second, and more importantly, they created a sizable population of women voters who could exert pressure on the national political parties. Now neither the Democrats nor the Republicans could afford to dismiss the issue of women's suffrage, because doing so might cost them the votes of angry female voters in the suffrage states.

Getting Radical

Up until the 1910s, the methods suffragists used to pursue the vote had mostly been polite and uncontroversial: they held meetings, circulated petitions, published newspapers, and called on politicians. But some activists began to feel that the movement was a little too polite, and argued that they could only achieve the goal of nationwide suffrage through more aggressive action. The person who spearheaded this approach was Alice Paul, who became one of the key figures in the passage of the Nineteenth Amendment (see biography on Paul, p. 122).

Paul's introduction to militant politics came in England, where radical suffragettes (the English term for suffragists) used disruptive demonstrations in seeking the vote. After arriving in Great Britain as a graduate student, Paul joined the protests, went to jail on numerous occasions, and engaged in

Thousands of protesters took to the streets of Washington, D.C., in March 1913 for this famous women's suffrage parade.

hunger strikes while behind bars. She returned to the United States in 1910, at the age of twenty-five. That same year she attended the NAWSA convention, where she explained the British approach to winning the vote. Paul soon began to advocate a similar approach in America. Her strategy—borrowed from the suffragettes—encouraged women to openly oppose the president and his party until he agreed to promote the enfranchisement of women.

Paul did not attempt to implement her plan immediately. Instead she asked the NAWSA leadership to send her to Washington, D.C., to lobby Congress. Anna Howard Shaw and her colleagues agreed to this plan, but they made it clear that Paul was responsible for raising her own money. Paul proved to be a tireless and extremely effective fundraiser, and she assembled a group of dedicated and relatively young activists to help her. Among them was Lucy Burns, a close friend of Paul who had also taken part in British suffrage protests.

Paul and her followers were particularly good at gaining publicity. In the early 1910s, suffragists had adopted the tactic of staging large-scale marches, and in March 1913 Paul's group put on the biggest parade of all. They jammed the streets of Washington with 8,000 female marchers from all across the country. But the procession turned out to be less notable for its size than for the violent altercations that took place. It was common for suffrage parades to be greeted by crowds of jeering men, but in Washington the insults turned to shoving, spitting, and physical assaults. Hundreds of participants suffered injuries. The inability or unwillingness of the police to protect the women resulted in a congressional investigation that cost the chief of police his job. The controversy provided the suffragists with lots of free publicity, most of which was positive. The Washington parade had coincided with the inauguration of President Woodrow Wilson. It turned out to be the first of many interactions between Alice Paul and the president.

Turmoil in the Movement

Paul's organization became known as the Congressional Union (CU), and it grew steadily in size. Though still a part of NAWSA, the CU began to steal attention away from its parent organization. This situation caused some bad feelings between the two groups, and the strain worsened when the two camps clashed over finances and tactics. In 1914 NAWSA and the CU formally separated. Paul's group then moved forward with her "opposition" plan for the congressional elections of 1914.

Because President Wilson was a Democrat, the Congressional Union actively opposed all Democratic candidates in the election—even those who had supported suffrage in the past. The CU focused on the nine western states where women then had the vote, which gave their message a real impact at the polls. Their colorful whistle-stop railroad campaign contributed to a number of Democratic losses, including twenty congressmen who had been considered friendly to the female vote.

The election results angered the leaders of NAWSA, who saw the Congressional Union's tactics as shortsighted and destructive to the suffrage cause. Paul and her group dismissed the criticism, declaring that politicians would never take suffrage seriously until they paid a political price for opposing it. They asserted that the Democrats' losses in Congress would force Wilson to explicitly support the suffrage cause.

In December 1915 Anna Howard Shaw resigned the presidency of NAWSA. She was replaced by Carrie Chapman Catt, who had served as NAWSA's president from 1900 to 1904 and later rejoined the association's leadership. Catt had a proven record as an organizer and innovator, and most

Dangerous Work

On March 25, 1911, a fire broke out at the Triangle Waist Company in New York City, a garment factory largely staffed by young immigrant women. As the workers attempted to flee the flames, they found the stairwell doors locked—a measure employed by factory owners to prevent theft. An outdoor fire escape collapsed under the weight of those trying to get away, leaving hundreds of workers trapped in the burning building. Some were killed directly by the smoke and flames. Others died when they leapt from the windows to escape the intense heat. More than 140 people lost their lives, almost all of them women. The tragedy helped convince many female workers that they needed the right to vote in order to help ensure their safety. A woman who survived the Triangle fire later remarked that "working women must use the ballot to in order to abolish the burning and crushing of our bodies for the profit of a very few."

members were happy to see her take the helm. Like her predecessor, however, Catt was on bad terms with Alice Paul and the CU. In early 1916 the two groups held a summit to discuss reuniting, but the divisions proved too wide to overcome. The meeting ended on a bad note. "All I wish to say is, I will fight you to the last ditch," Catt told Paul as she departed. The suffrage movement was now permanently divided into two groups.

In some ways the division of the suffrage movement seemed like a replay of the split between the NWSA and AWSA back in the 1800s. This time, however, it proved beneficial to the cause. Though the two groups did not plot strategy together, their actions ended up complementing one another. The CU soon evolved into the National Woman's Party, and its members became the militant wing of the suffrage movement. They were willing to employ controversial tactics and endure great discomforts to draw attention to the cause.

Under Catt, meanwhile, NAWSA became a highly efficient, centralized organization with a well-plotted strategy for winning the vote. In addition, its more reasonable tone and more respectable image kept the suffragists from being dismissed as extremists. For all their differences, the two groups had a similar organizational structure: both were led by powerful women who sometimes faced criticism for being autocratic but also inspired strong devotion from their followers.

The Winning Plan

In the late summer of 1916, the members of NAWSA gathered in Atlantic City, New Jersey, for their annual convention. Some of the delegates may have arrived expecting to enjoy the boardwalk and beaches, but this turned out to be the most serious NAWSA gathering in years. Just nine months into her term as president, Carrie Chapman Catt was about to outline a new course of action for the association. Its ambitious goals were clear in the name that Catt gave it: "the Winning Plan."

NAWSA's preparation for the new push had begun months earlier. Catt had replaced the group's executive board with members she personally selected for their sharp political skills. Then she settled the question of tactics. For years, NAWSA's focus had wavered between the state campaigns for suffrage and the nationwide passage of the Susan B. Anthony Amendment. From the 1890s until the early 1910s, the group had placed more emphasis on the state activities. Now, however, Alice Paul's congressional lobbying had re-energized the fight for the amendment. In fact, the Susan B. Anthony Amendment had come up for votes in the Senate in 1914 and in the House in 1915, but it had fallen far short of the necessary two-thirds majority in both instances. Catt decided to put NAWSA "securely on the Amendment trolley," believing that the federal mandate was the quickest way for all American women to achieve the vote. In a letter to a colleague, Catt noted that, until that point, NAWSA "never really has worked for the Federal Amendment…. If it should once do it, there is no knowing what might happen."

NAWSA rolled out an arsenal of new weapons to aid in the fight for the amendment. The group overhauled its Congressional Committee in Washington, D.C., placing it under the direction of Maud Wood Park. Known as the Front Door Lobby, Park's group took over a mansion, dubbed Suffrage House, where the lobbyists lived as well as worked. The association also moved its publicity campaign to Washington. This effort, controlled by the Leslie Bureau of Suffrage Education, boasted a staff of twenty-five journalists and public-relations specialists.

The key to all of these new efforts was money. The NAWSA treasury, which had been building gradually over the previous decade, was now

The Woman on the Horse

Inez Milholland

The famous 1913 suffrage parade in Washington, D.C., was led by a striking woman in a white cloak atop a white horse. This conspicuous figure was Inez Milholland (also known as Inez Milholland Boissevain), a lawyer with socialist political beliefs who had begun working with Alice Paul the year before. As memorable as she was on horseback that day, Milholland went on to play a larger role in the fight for suffrage.

An electrifying public speaker, Milholland became a vital part of many rallies. During the 1916 election campaign, she embarked on a grueling tour of the western states—despite the fact that she was suffering from tonsillitis and pernicious anemia. In late October, Milholland collapsed while speaking before a crowd in Los Angeles. According to legend, she had just uttered the phrase, "How long must women wait for liberty?" when she fainted.

Milholland died a month later, and she quickly became a martyr for women's suffrage. Supporters held an emotional memorial service in her honor in December 1916. "We got up this memorial meeting in the capitol and sent a message from the memorial meeting to President Wilson urging that no more sacrifices like this be made necessary in the effort to get the enfranchisement of women," Alice Paul remembered in *Conversations with Alice Paul: Woman Suffrage and the Equal Rights Amendment*.

The memory of Milholland's sacrifice galvanized the radical suffragists in their 1917 protests. Fellow suffragist Ruth Fitch immortalized Milholland and the romantic glory she came to symbolize in the following poem:

> Your gallant youth,
> Your glorious self-sacrifice—all ours!
> Inez, vibrant, courageous, symbolic,
> Death cannot claim you!

brought into play. The organization also received several important new sources of funding. For example, when Mrs. Frank Leslie, widow of the founder of Leslie's Illustrated Newspaper, died in 1914, she gave Catt more than $900,000 in cash and property for the suffrage cause. Leslie's jewelry collection alone was worth nearly $35,000, and the proceeds from its sale were used to finance the suffrage education bureau that was named after her. Catt claimed that NAWSA spent a total of one million dollars a year in the late 1910s, which was a sizable amount at the time.

Under the Winning Plan, Catt and her executive board concentrated the organization's power in their own hands, and they decided how and where suffrage battles would be fought. They did not abandon campaigns for state suffrage—several were waged in the late 1910s, and four states (including New York) enfranchised women during this period—but the national organization called the shots. The executive board also directed most of the lobbying and publicity efforts carried out by local chapters. Their detailed plans and professionally produced written materials created a unified message all across the country. Continuing the trend that had started in the late 1800s, NAWSA once again narrowed its focus. Amending the Constitution became the group's single goal. As Catt declared, "We do not care a 'ginger snap' about anything but that Federal Amendment."

Chapter Seven

WINNING THE VOTE

The avenue is misty gray,
And here beside the guarded gate
We hold our golden blowing flags
And wait.

—Beulah Amidon, "On the Picket Line"

Did you expect us to turn back? We never turn back ... and
we won't until Democracy is won.

—National Woman's Party member Elsie Hill

The same year that NAWSA President Carrie Chapman Catt put her "Winning Plan" into action, the United States prepared for a presidential election. The incumbent, Democrat Woodrow Wilson, faced a tough opponent in Republican Charles E. Hughes. During his first term as president, Wilson had taken a middle-of-the-road position on women's suffrage (see biography on Wilson, p. 140). He said that he personally favored granting women the right to vote, but felt that the matter should be decided on a state-by-state basis rather than imposed by a constitutional amendment.

As the 1916 election approached, Alice Paul's radical suffrage group—now known as the National Woman's Party (NWP)—put its "opposition" plan into motion once again. Since the president had failed to endorse the Susan B. Anthony Amendment, Paul and her followers actively campaigned against Wilson and his party. The NWP's efforts failed to swing the election, though, as Wilson won reelection in a close race.

Paul and her colleagues felt that they could not wait until the next major election to apply further pressure. They discussed their options with Harriot Stanton Blatch, an advisor to the NWP who agreed that more extreme mea-

Members of the National Woman's Party picket in front of the White House to demand voting rights.

sures were needed. "We can't organize bigger and more influential deputations [groups]," Blatch explained. "We can't organize bigger processions. We can't, women, do anything more in that line. We have got to take a new departure." The action they came up with provided a key turning point in the battle for women's suffrage: they took the fight, literally, to the president's front door.

On January 10, 1917, a group of women arrived at the gates of the White House. They carried the purple, white, and gold banners that had become the symbol of the NWP. They also carried signs reading "Mr. President, What Will You Do For Woman Suffrage?" and "How Long Must Women Wait For Liberty?" With this action, the National Woman's Party began picketing the president's residence.

Although this type of direct protest at the White House would become commonplace in later years, it was unheard of in 1917. Despite the startling nature of their activities, however, the picketers initially were received with tolerance. President Wilson often nodded as he passed, and he even expressed concern about the women's welfare during particularly cold weather. "Go out there and ask those ladies if they won't come in and get warm," Wilson reportedly told the White House's head usher. "And if they come, see that they have some hot tea and coffee." The usher returned to report that the picketers had "indignantly refused" the president's offer.

The rationale behind the picketing was straightforward: the NWP believed the president had enough influence to push the suffrage amendment through Congress, and the organization's leaders intended to keep confronting him until he agreed to do so. Alice Paul explained the process with an analogy: "If a creditor stands before a man's house all day long, demanding payment of his bill, the man must either remove the creditor or pay the bill." The president made no attempt to remove the protesters during the winter of 1917, but that would soon change.

World War I

Beginning in 1914, Europe's great powers had become locked in a bloody war. The United States remained neutral through the early years of the conflict, but in 1917 it became difficult for America to remain on the sidelines. Between the end of January and the beginning of April, a series of events brought the United States closer and closer to joining the fray. Finally, on April 2, President Wilson asked Congress to declare war against Germany. Four days later America officially entered World War I.

Both NAWSA and the NWP now had to decide if they should alter their efforts because of the war. Many suffragists looked back on the example of the Civil War, when women's rights activists had agreed to suspend their activities once hostilities began. Some blamed that pause for the difficulties that the women's suffrage movement had faced in the postwar era. Both Carrie Chapman Catt and Alice Paul called together their respective executive councils to consider the question.

NAWSA decided to continue its campaign for the vote. "This is the time for speeding up," Catt stated, "not resting." At the same time, the organization vowed to support the war effort by performing patriotic service, such as aiding the Red Cross and selling War Savings Stamps. The idea behind these efforts was to show that women were loyal Americans and thus deserved the right to vote.

The NWP also decided to continue its suffrage work during the war. But for Alice Paul and her colleagues, this decision meant that *all* of their work would continue—including the White House protests. It turned out to be a very controversial decision. Before the war, average Americans had viewed the picketing as somewhat startling and perhaps mildly inappropriate. With the nation involved in a war, however, some people considered the NWP's actions unpatriotic and even treasonous. Even a number of prominent people within the suffrage movement—including Harriot Stanton Blatch—voiced disapproval of the continued White House protests during a time of war. "Our *own women* ... began to revolt against us," Paul recalled years later.

Arrests and Hunger Strikes

The NWP leaders remained undaunted in the face of criticism. The picketing continued in wartime, and the protestors began carrying special banners aimed at foreign dignitaries who visited the White House. The most famous banner addressed diplomats from Russia, a country that had just given the vote to women. It read, in part, "The women of America tell you that America is not a democracy.... Tell our government that it must liberate its women before it can claim free Russia as an ally."

Meanwhile, the atmosphere outside the White House turned increasingly hostile. Crowds of angry onlookers—many of them off-duty members of the military—shouted insults at the picketers. Banners were ripped from their hands and torn to pieces. Shoving matches erupted. In late June a member of the Washington police force contacted Alice Paul to deliver an ultimatum. "He wanted to warn us that if anybody did go out again on the picket line, it would be their duty to arrest us," Paul recalled. "I just remember having a

NWP picketers faced hostility from onlookers and arrest by police during the White House demonstrations.

long consultation, 'well what should we do?'… Then we just deliberately took about six women … that were *willing* to be arrested and who wouldn't cave in if they were arrested. And they started out."

On June 22, 1917, Lucy Burns and another picketer were placed under arrest and charged with obstructing traffic. (This charge made little sense, since it was not illegal for the protesters to gather on the sidewalk, but the authorities used it anyway.) The police hoped to scare the picketers away from the White House by arresting them, but the tactic failed. Each day more women returned to the picket lines, and each day they were taken to jail. Over the next several months, about 500 women were arrested for picketing, some of them multiple times.

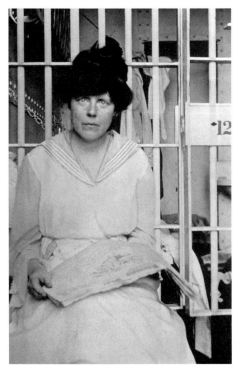

Lucy Burns was one of the suffrage protesters who spent time in prison for her actions.

Initially, the women were released without penalty or after serving three-day jail sentences. Before long, however, the district court judge lost patience with the protestors. In July he began handing out sixty-day terms in a workhouse. These stiff sentences created bad publicity for the president, so Wilson attempted to defuse the situation by issuing a pardon for all of the prisoners. It proved to be only a temporary pause in the battle. "We're very much obliged to the President for pardoning the pickets," Alice Paul said, "but we'll be picketing again next Monday. The President can pardon us again if we're arrested on Monday, and again and again, but …picketing will continue and sooner or later he will have to do something about it."

August saw a number of riots break out at the White House gates. The picketers were attacked by mobs of counter protestors and, on occasion, by the police themselves. A shot was even fired into the NWP headquarters in Washington by an unknown assailant, though no one was wounded. Meanwhile, the arrests and harsh sentences continued, and for many months Wilson made no further effort to intervene. More than 160 women served time in prison for picketing. Most of them were held in the Occuquan Workhouse, which was located outside of Washington. Conditions there were typical of most prisons of the era—in other words, very difficult. The air was bad, the rooms infested with rats and insects, the food filled with worms. (See "Picketing and Prison: The Experiences of Ernestine Hara Kettler," p. 184.) In an incident that became known as the "Night of Terror," prison guards physically abused some of the suffragist prisoners, beating and choking them and refusing to treat the injured.

By the fall of 1917, the NWP prisoners decided to adopt more extreme measures. Borrowing another tactic from the British suffragettes, they undertook a hunger strike. One of the most extreme forms of nonviolent protest, a hunger strike forces a jailer to make a choice: give in to a prisoner's demands, or eventually have the prisoner die of starvation. The hunger strike coincided with the imprisonment of Paul herself. Arrested at the White House on October 20, she received the longest sentence of any of the suffragists—seven months. She became one of the initial hunger strikers at Occuquan, as did NWP member Rose Winslow (see sidebar "Notes from a Hunger Striker," p. 82).

In November, sixteen more prisoners began hunger strikes. Not wishing to give in to the women, the Occuquan officials resorted to forcibly feeding them through rubber tubes. Dorothy Day, one of the hunger strikers, found the ordeal far from glorious. "To lie there through the long day, to feel the nausea and emptiness of hunger," she wrote, "I lost all consciousness of any cause—I had no sense of being a radical, making protest against a government, carrying on a non-violent revolution. I could only feel darkness and desolation all around me." Paul, however, saw the hunger

President Woodrow Wilson finally agreed to support the Susan B. Anthony Amendment in 1918.

strikes as a way to move the suffrage cause forward. "It's happened rather well," she wrote in a letter, "because we'll have ammunition against the [Wilson] Administration, and the more harsh and repressive they seem, the better."

The Power of Cooperation

In the meantime, NAWSA was using more conventional means to pursue the vote. At the outset of World War I, Congress had postponed consideration of all legislation that was not related to the war effort. This emphasis on war measures put the suffrage amendment on the back burner, but NAWSA continued to work quietly behind the scenes. The group even had some success in convincing politicians that suffrage *was* a war measure. President Wilson came to agree with this idea in 1918, stating that "I regard the extension of suffrage to women as vitally essential to the successful prosecution of the great war of humanity in which we are engaged."

Notes from a Hunger Striker

Rose Winslow was one of the National Woman's Party members who conducted a prison hunger strike in 1917 and was subjected to forced feedings. During the ordeal, she recorded her thoughts on small pieces of paper that were later smuggled out of prison.

The women are all so magnificent, so beautiful. Alice Paul is as thin as ever, pale and large-eyed. We have been in solitary for five weeks. There is nothing to tell but that the days go by somehow. I have felt quite feeble for the last few days—faint, so that I could hardly get my hair brushed, my arms ached so. But to-day I am well again....

* * * *

[To her husband:—]

My fainting probably means nothing except that I am not strong after these weeks. I know you won't be alarmed....

The place is alive with roaches, crawling all over the walls, everywhere. I found one in my bed the other day....

* * * *

Alice Paul is in the psychopathic ward. She dreaded forcible feeding frightfully, and I hate to think how she must be feeling. I had a nervous time of it, gasping a long time afterward, and my stomach rejecting during the process. I spent a bad, restless night, but otherwise I am all right. The poor soul who fed me got liberally besprinkled during the process. I heard myself making the most hideous sounds.... One feels so forsaken when one lies prone and people shove a pipe down one's stomach....

* * * *

Yesterday was bad day for me in feeding. I was vomiting continually during the process. The tube has developed an irritation somewhere that is painful....

* * * *

I fainted again last night. I just fell flop over in the bathroom where I was washing my hands and was led to bed when I recovered, by a nurse. I lost consciousness just as I got there again. I felt horribly faint until 12 o'clock, then fell asleep for awhile....

* * * *

Don't let them tell you we take this well. Miss Paul vomits much. I do, too, except when I'm not nervous, as I have been every time against my will. I try to be less feeble-minded. It's the nervous reaction, and I can't control it much. I don't imagine bathing one's food in tears very good for one.

We think of the coming feeding all day. It is horrible. The doctor thinks I take it well. I hate the thought of Alice Paul and the others if I take it well.

* * * *

I am really all right. If this continues very long I perhaps won't be. I am interested to see how long our so-called 'splendid American men' will stand for this form of discipline....

All the officers here know we are making this hunger strike that women fighting for liberty may be considered political prisoners; we have told them. God knows we don't want other women ever to have to do this over again.

Source: Stevens, Doris. *Jailed for Freedom*. New York: Boni and Liveright, 1920.

Confronting the President

The presidential protests staged by the National Woman's Party were intricate operations. The following account describes a demonstration that took place at the U.S. Capitol in December 1916:

> Early that morning, before the outer doors were opened, five women of the Congressional Union appeared before the Capitol. After a long wait the doors were opened, and—the first of a big crowd—they placed themselves in the front row of the gallery just to the left of the big clock. They faced the Speaker's desk, from which the President would read his message.... Mabel Vernon sat in the middle of the five women. Pinned to her skirt, under the enveloping cape that she wore, was a big banner of yellow sateen.... Mabel Vernon unpinned the banner and dropped it, all ready for unrolling, on the floor.... At the psychological moment, which had been picked beforehand,... Mabel Vernon whispered the series of signals which had previously been decided on. Immediately—working like a beautifully co-ordinated machine—the five women stooped, lifted the banner, and, holding it tightly by the tapes, dropped it over the balcony edge. It unrolled with a smart snap and displayed these words:
>
> MR. PRESIDENT, WHAT WILL YOU DO FOR WOMAN SUFFRAGE?...
>
> The effect was instantaneous. The President looked up, hesitated a moment, then went on reading. All the Congressmen turned. The Speaker sat motionless. A buzz ran wildly across the floor.
>
> Source: Inez Hayes Irwin, *The Story of Alice Paul and the National Woman's Party*, Fairfax, Va.: Denlinger's, 1977.

NAWSA also worked feverishly at the state level. In November 1917 the activists scored a key win in New York, where voters passed a suffrage referendum. At long last an eastern state had given women the ballot, which helped convince politicians all over the country that women's suffrage enjoyed widespread support. NAWSA leaders were ecstatic at the victory.

At the same time, though, they felt dismayed about the events taking place in Washington, D.C. Catt and her colleagues bitterly opposed the direct actions of the NWP. They believed that the protests and arrests discredited the voting-rights movement and hurt NAWSA's lobbying work in Congress. In response, NAWSA went in the opposite direction from the NWP, expressing strong support for President Wilson and denouncing the militant actions of the protestors. Catt called the White House pickets "an unwarranted discourtesy to the President and a futile annoyance to the members of Congress." NAWSA formally asked the NWP to end the protests but, not surprisingly, this request had no effect.

NAWSA's image as the reasonable, well-behaved wing of the suffrage movement became increasingly important as the government's standoff with the NWP continued. The picketing, prison terms, and hunger strikes created a lot of negative publicity for the president and his Democratic Party. They began to realize that the only practical way to end the crisis was to support the suffrage amendment. Yet the president did not want to create the appearance of caving in to the radicals. The presence of NAWSA gave him a way out of the crisis. As historian Christine A. Lunardini points out in *From Equal Suffrage to Equal Rights*, "NAWSA became, in Wilson's view particularly, the moderates, the representatives of real American womanhood." The president ultimately took steps that met the demands of the NWP, but he publicly attributed these steps to the lobbying efforts of NAWSA. Wilson thus managed to save face and still bring the protests to an end.

Progress became visible in late September 1917. The U.S. House of Representatives agreed to create a Committee on Woman Suffrage—an important step toward bringing the Susan B. Anthony Amendment to a vote once again. President Wilson gave his blessing to the plan of establishing a committee, which seemed to indicate that he was becoming a cautious supporter of the amendment.

Another breakthrough came in late November, when a journalist named David Lawrence, who was a close friend of President Wilson, visited Alice Paul in prison. Though he claimed to be acting in an unofficial capacity, Lawrence hinted that the president might be able to bring about congressional action on the suffrage amendment. A few days later, all of the jailed protesters were released. Shortly thereafter, the Rules Committee of the House of Representatives announced that the amendment would be brought up for a vote on January 10, 1918. Although it never became clear whether Wilson and Paul had officially struck a deal, the crisis over the White House protests suddenly eased. With real progress being made toward passage of the amendment, the picketers suspended their activities at the presidential residence.

Amending the Constitution

On the three previous occasions that Congress had voted on the Susan B. Anthony Amendment, the measure had fallen far short of the two-thirds approval needed for passage. The suffrage cause had gained ground since the last vote was taken in 1915, but a lot of doubt still existed as to whether the amendment would receive the necessary support in its first test—in the U.S. House of Representatives. At this crucial moment, Woodrow Wilson threw his full support behind the amendment. On the day before the vote, the president called a group of twelve undecided legislators to the White House and told them that enfranchising women was "an act of right and justice." Wilson's support proved decisive. All twelve of the legislators voted in favor of the amendment, and the House approved the amendment with just barely a two-thirds majority—274 votes in favor, 136 against. The first hurdle had been cleared.

The NWP's opposition strategy had been based on the idea that President Wilson had the political power to push the amendment through Congress. Events in the House of Representatives seemed to prove their point. But the suffragists soon learned that the president's power was not unlimited. In the Senate, legislators opposed to the bill succeeded in slowing its progress. When the vote finally took place on October 1, 1918, even a last-minute address from the president could not turn the tide. The measure fell two votes short of passage.

Although this result dealt the suffragists yet another disappointment, they did not consider it a crushing defeat. With congressional elections about to take place, they knew that the addition of just a few pro-suffrage senators could bring them victory the following year. And that is exactly what came to pass. Effective campaigns by NAWSA led to the defeat of two anti-suffrage senators in the November 1918 election. The election results not only improved the pro-suffrage vote count, but also sent a warning to other sena-

Congresswoman Rankin

Jeannette Rankin

While female *voters* had always been the suffragists' primary concern, in 1916 they had the pleasure of witnessing another product of the women's rights movement: the first female member of the U.S. Congress. Jeanette Rankin, a former NAWSA activist from Montana, was elected to the U.S. House of Representatives that year. On April 2, 1917, Carrie Chapman Catt and other suffragists proudly accompanied Rankin to her first legislative session at the Capitol.

That evening, Congress voted on the declaration of war against Germany, and Rankin received a lesson in the difficulties of politics. A pacifist, she chose to vote against the war. This single decision was a major reason why she was voted out of office in 1918. Strangely, Rankin got a chance to relive this experience twenty-four years later. After being reelected to Congress in 1940, she faced another vote on a declaration of war. Rankin stuck with her conscience and voted against the United States entering World War II—an extremely lonely position in the wake of the Japanese attack on Pearl Harbor. As before, she lost her House seat in the next election.

tors that they might face a future election defeat if they failed to vote for the amendment.

When Congress reconvened in 1919, the Susan B. Anthony Amendment was once again approved by the House, then brought to the Senate for a vote in early June. By this point, World War I had come to an end. But the fact that the amendment could no longer be promoted as a war measure did not seem to reduce its support. With President Wilson again applying strong pressure, the amendment passed in the Senate by a vote of 56 to 25. The Susan B. Anthony Amendment now became known as the proposed Nineteenth

Alice Paul (third from left) sews the thirty-sixth star on the NWP's ratification banner, signifying the successful addition of the Nineteenth Amendment to the Constitution.

Amendment. If approved by three-fourths of the states—a total of thirty-six—it would become part of the United States Constitution.

Ratification by the States

Both NAWSA and the NWP established suffrage ratification committees all across the country. These committees applied the same sophisticated lobbying and publicity tactics that the parent organizations had developed in Washington, D.C. The first victories came almost immediately. The legislatures of Michigan and Wisconsin ratified the amendment only a week after its approval by the Senate. More states followed throughout 1919 and into 1920. To keep track of the amendment's progress, Alice Paul created a large banner on which she sewed a star for each state that had ratified it. She added the thirty-fifth star in March 1920, when Washington's legislature approved the measure.

The suffragists were just one state shy of their goal, but finding that final state to ratify the amendment was no easy task. State legislators in the Deep South largely opposed the amendment, so the activists mounted no serious effort to secure ratification there. Several states in the Northeast seemingly offered better chances for passage, but they all proved to be disappointments for the suffragists. By the summer of 1920, the situation was growing tense. As often happens in the years immediately following a war, the country seemed to be taking on a conservative mood. Catt and other suffrage leaders feared that if they did not secure the final state soon, they might end up wait-ing several more years, or perhaps longer. They thus turned their attention to a state that was considered far from a sure thing—Tennessee.

Once a part of the rebellious Confederacy, Tennessee shared some of the conservative attitudes and distrust of federal initiatives shown by its Southern neighbors. But suffragists felt encouraged by the fact that the Tennessee legis-lature was willing to hold a special session to consider the amendment. They hoped that this indicated that the state also had some progressive sentiment. This mix of opinions led to a dramatic showdown.

As the August session of the Tennessee legislature got underway, suffrage supporters flooded into the state to try to influence the vote. So did anti-suf-fragists from the National Association Opposed to Woman Suffrage and the Southern Women's League for the Rejection of the Susan B. Anthony Amend-ment. The antis were intent on mounting a last-ditch effort to derail the amendment. The decision hinged on a final vote in the Tennessee State Sen-ate. The legislators cast their votes on August 18. An initial poll to "table" or dismiss the amendment came out 48 votes in favor, and 48 against. The tie meant that a final vote would have to be taken. If it, too, ended in a tie, the amendment would not be ratified.

A packed gallery watched as the roll-call vote took place. Senator after senator stayed true to his earlier position, and it looked as if a tie was inevitable. Then the speaker called the name of twenty-four-year-old Senator Harry Burn. Burn had previously voted to table the amendment, and he wore a red rose in his lapel—the symbol of the anti-suffragists (suffragists, on the other hand, wore yellow roses). To everyone's surprise, Burn stood up, threw his red rose to the floor, and voted in favor of the amendment. His vote broke the tie, and Tennessee became the thirty-sixth state to ratify the Nineteenth Amendment. Burn later explained that he had changed his mind because his mother had urged him to support the amendment. "I know that a mother's advice is always safest for her boy to follow," he said, "and my mother wanted me to vote for ratification."

Some procedural and legal wrangling delayed the state's final approval, but the governor of Tennessee finally mailed the certificate of ratification to Washington, D.C., on August 24. When it arrived two days later—on August 26, 1920—the U.S. Secretary of State declared that the Nineteenth Amendment was part of the United States Constitution. At the NWP headquarters, Alice Paul added the final star to the ratification banner and unfurled it over the outdoor balcony. A little more than 72 years after the suffrage pioneers had launched the movement at the Seneca Falls Convention, their dream of gaining the right to vote for all American women finally became a reality.

Chapter Eight

THE LEGACY OF WOMEN'S SUFFRAGE

Our successors ... have big work before them—much bigger,
in fact, than they imagine. We are only the stone that started
the ripple, but they are the ripple that is spreading and will
eventually cover the whole pond.

—Elizabeth Cady Stanton

For decades, both suffragists and their opponents had predicted that immense changes would take place if women were allowed to vote. Those opposed to enfranchising women warned that female voters would threaten the basic social fabric of the country, while optimistic suffragists claimed that they would help solve society's more stubborn problems. As it turned out, both claims were exaggerated. Nevertheless, women's suffrage remains an extremely important development in the nation's history.

Passage of the Nineteenth Amendment is significant, first of all, because it brought one of America's most dearly held democratic principles—that all citizens should have an active voice in their government—closer to reality. As Anne Firor Scott and Andrew MacKay Scott explained in *One Half the People*:

> Why did women deserve the vote? Not because they would use
> it to remake the world or advance their own interests but
> because they were entitled to it. If one accepts the central
> democratic principle, consent of the governed, then women
> should have the vote and participate in the decisions of govern-
> ment under which they live. All other arguments are secondary.

Judged by the millions of potential voters it brought into the electorate, the Nineteenth Amendment ranks among the largest changes ever made to the nation's election laws. It was the last major initiative of this kind until the 1960s, when the civil rights movement finally forced lawmakers to address the disenfranchisement of African Americans. The Twenty-fourth Amendment, passed in 1964, eliminated poll taxes (the practice of charging voters fees to cast their ballots) in federal and presidential elections, while the Voting Rights Acts of 1965, 1970, and 1975 outlawed other discriminatory election practices that had been widespread in the South. Another electoral change took place in 1971 with the passage of the Twenty-sixth Amendment, which lowered the minimum voting age to eighteen.

For the men and women who framed these later measures, the Nineteenth Amendment provided an example of legislation that addressed inequities in voting practices. But considering the amount of time that elapsed between the passage of women's suffrage and the later amendments and laws, it is safe to say that the Nineteenth Amendment did not create an immediate groundswell of support for further electoral changes.

The methods the suffragists used in winning the vote added to the significance of the Nineteenth Amendment. The women who called for equal suffrage found themselves in a difficult situation. They demanded a voice in government, yet their demands were easily dismissed because they had no voice in government. "It is difficult to imagine how powerless women were without the vote," noted historian Suzanne M. Marilley in her study of the suffrage movement. "No elected official had to listen to any woman's suggestion for legislative reform." As a result, the suffrage activists had to develop innovative ways of overcoming their lack of political might.

In *The Ideas of the Woman Suffrage Movement, 1890-1920,* Aileen S. Kraditor describes the fight for the vote as a case study in "how a group without political power could obtain such power from those who already have it." The suffragists came up with a variety of new methods to promote their agenda and learned to leverage the small amounts of power they were able to accumulate. In fact, the sophisticated lobbying techniques pioneered by the National American Woman Suffrage Association (NAWSA) in the early 1900s remain part of pressure-group politics today. Similarly, the confrontational activities of the National Woman's Party (NWP) introduced new techniques of nonviolent protest to the U.S. political arena, some of which would be employed by civil-rights and antiwar demonstrators later in the twentieth century.

Longtime suffragist Carrie Chapman Catt (center) exercises her right to vote for the first time during the 1920 presidential election.

Women's Suffrage and American Politics

In the eight decades since the passage of the Nineteenth Amendment, historians have engaged in spirited debate about the effect of female voters in the political arena. Some scholars, such as Judith Shklar in *American Citizenship: The Quest for Inclusion,* have argued that women produced "no noticeable political change at all." According to this view, the American political system stayed much the same after women began participating in it. While the claim that women voters made absolutely no change is arguable, historians generally agree that there were few large-scale differences in voting patterns and no major shake-up in the American political system following passage of the Nineteenth Amendment.

Many observers—and many of the suffragists themselves—had expected that the sudden inclusion of millions of new voters would alter politics tremendously. To bring about sweeping changes, however, large numbers of women

93

would have had to act together to form a cohesive political bloc that would support particular candidates and issues. This kind of widespread unity failed to develop. American women, like American men, came from a wide variety of backgrounds and had different priorities and opinions. In this way, it is hardly surprising that they would seek different political goals. As historian Nancy F. Cott wrote in her essay "Across the Great Divide," "Given the divisions among women and given the nature of the political system, a women's voting bloc—or, even the possibility of a lobbying bloc representing *all* women—must be considered an interpretive fiction rather than a realistic expectation."

While most historians admit that women's suffrage did not produce wholesale changes, some believe that female voters did have an impact on certain political issues. Anne Firor Scott and Andrew MacKay Scott contend that "one must be uninformed to argue that the ballot did not materially help women to advance their most urgent causes." They suggest, for example, that women were an important factor in enacting such liberal reforms as the Equal Pay Act of 1963, the Civil Rights Act of 1964, and affirmative action policies.

Other historians see women's impact changing over time. They note that in the first years after passage of the Nineteenth Amendment, the addition of female voters helped bring about several new laws. One example was the Sheppard-Towner Maternity and Infancy Act of 1921, an early social welfare program that provided federal money for children's health care. Some historians believe that women also played a role in the passage of the far-reaching social reforms of the 1930s, including the Social Security Act.

On the other hand, some historians believe that women's influence declined in the late 1920s. This decline may be partially attributed to the changing nature of the major women's advocacy groups. Shortly after succeeding in its mission of passing the Nineteenth Amendment, NAWSA transformed into the National League of Women Voters (NLWV). When founding the group, Carrie Chapman Catt described it as a "semi-political body." In fact, the NLWV became less active as a political force over the course of the 1920s and instead emphasized nonpartisan, educational initiatives. These activities were designed to help women become responsible voters without pushing a certain agenda—a valuable service given the number of women who were unfamiliar with the details of elections and politics.

At the same time that the NLWV withdrew from shaping public policy, increasing numbers of women joined the traditional political parties. Catt

American citizens showed a renewed interest in women's rights during the women's liberation movement of the 1970s.

favored this process, as well, arguing that "the only way to get things done is to get them done on the inside of a political party." Many observers believe that women's voices grew weaker once they entered the existing parties, however. Some argue that female influence remained low until the 1960s and 1970s, when such women's rights groups as the National Organization for Women (NOW) became powerful.

Some historians point to the failure of the Equal Rights Amendment as evidence of women's declining political influence. The NWP first proposed this constitutional measure in 1923. It stated simply that "men and women shall have equal rights throughout the United States." But the ERA failed to gain the vocal support that had been given to the Nineteenth Amendment. Many women's groups, including the NLWV, initially opposed the ERA because they

Supporters of the Equal Rights Amendment carry a banner down Pennsylvania Avenue in Washington, D.C., in 1977.

felt it would undermine some of the workplace protections that women had previously won. In addition, the NWP was a much smaller and less powerful group by the 1920s, so it had limited success in promoting the amendment.

Still, the NWP—and Alice Paul in particular—never gave up on the measure. When the women's rights movement strengthened in the 1960s, passing the ERA became a priority. In 1972 Congress finally approved the amendment, but it failed to be ratified by the necessary number of states within the seven-year time limit that was placed on the process. The amendment has been reintroduced in each session of Congress, but it has received little attention from politicians in the conservative political atmosphere that has prevailed since the 1980s.

Voting Trends

Some scholars have attempted to gauge women's political input by tracking voter participation. In the first few decades after passage of the Nineteenth Amendment, the percentage of women who participated in elections was lower than the percentage of men. These findings led critics to charge that women truly did not want the vote, as the anti-suffragists had claimed. But historians contend that the low initial turnout among female voters was not surprising, given the fact that women were unfamiliar with the political process. As Mark Lawrence Kornbluh explained in *Why America Stopped Voting,* women "had not been socialized into electoral politics."

Overall, the entry of women never sparked the societal upheaval and discord predicted by anti-suffrage forces. In *The Right to Vote*, Alexander Keyssar asserted that such factors as culture and class have proven more decisive than sex in the way people vote. "Women certainly were empowered by enfranchisement," Keyssar wrote, "and their lives consequently (if gradually) may have changed in a host of different ways, but they tended to vote for the same parties and candidates that their husbands, fathers, and brothers supported."

This predilection for following the voting example of male household members gradually fell to the wayside, however, as women voters gained greater confidence in their own abilities. Meanwhile, voting participation levels among men and women became almost even during the 1970s. By the late 1980s women had surpassed men by a small margin, a trend that continued through the 2004 elections. It is important to note, however, that the percentage of both men and women who exercise their right to vote has dropped markedly during the past 100 years. The percentage of the adult population voting in presidential elections has ranged from 50 to 60 percent since the 1920s. Between 1840 and 1900, by contrast, turnout ranged between 75 and 80 percent.

Another way to track women's political participation is to examine trends in the number of female candidates and elected officials. Very few women held political office in the 1920s. Their numbers have increased significantly in the decades since, but men continue to hold far more elective positions than women, and the number of female officeholders lags far behind the proportion of women in the overall population. According to recent estimates by the U.S. Census Bureau, nearly 51 percent of the country's population is female. Yet statistics provided by the Center for American Women and Politics for 2005 show that women held just 15 percent of seats in the U.S. Congress, about 25 percent of state elective offices, and about 20 percent of state legislative offices. These figures suggest that the political power and influence of women continues to lag behind that of men.

In January 2005 Condoleezza Rice (right) became Secretary of State in the administration of President George W. Bush (left). Rice thus became the first African-American woman in U.S. history to occupy that important cabinet post.

Nonetheless, women have assumed ever more prominent and influential positions in American government in recent decades. In 1984 Geraldine Ferraro became the first female candidate for vice president of the United States, and nine years later Carol Moseley-Braun of Illinois became the first African-American female to serve in the U.S. Senate. Madeleine Albright ascended to the highest government office thus far held by a woman in 1997, when she was sworn in as U.S. Secretary of State. In 2003 a record-setting fourteen women were seated in the U.S. Senate as part of the 108th Congress, and in 2005 Condoleezza Rice became the second female Secretary of State, and the first African American woman to hold this position. By this same time twenty-one states had elected a female governor, and a record nine women held the highest office in their states in 2005.

The Impact of Women's Suffrage on Society

Political change is not the only measure of the impact of the women's suffrage movement. Historians note that women, in the process of fighting for and gaining electoral rights, also advanced the cause of gender equality in virtually every aspect of American society and culture. The scope of those changes is striking when judged against the conditions that existed in the mid-1800s, when the suffrage movement began. At that time, women's opportunities for social interaction and education were extremely limited. By the time suffrage was granted, conditions had improved significantly on both counts. The campaign for the vote in the late 1800s and early 1900s brought women more forcefully into public roles and proved that they were capable of taking on more than the traditional domestic responsibilities. In short, winning the vote was an essential first step toward empowering women, affirming their abilities, and allowing them to confidently pursue new opportunities in business and education (women now account for the majority of students earning advanced college degrees in the United States). As Aileen S. Kraditor explained in *Ideas of the Woman Suffrage Movement, 1890-1920,* many women "became suffragists partly because of the intense shame they felt at being thought unfit to help govern their own country. When they acquired that right they felt a new pride in American democracy and a new respect for themselves."

The achieving of women's suffrage also paved the way for other gender-related reform movements that came later. Most notable was the resurgence in women's rights activism that took place in the 1960s and 1970s. Often termed women's liberation or "women's lib," the movement pursued many of the ideas that had been advanced by the more radical feminist activists of the 1800s and early 1900s. In general, that meant pursuing more equal treatment for women in a broad range of social, professional, and political areas. While the legislative centerpiece of the movement—the Equal Rights Amendment—failed to be enacted, the impact of women's liberation on society has been immense. The vast majority of occupations are now open to women as well as men, even careers in areas such as the military that were unimaginable to women of the 1950s and 1960s. Overall, a great deal of progress has been made toward eliminating sexism in media depictions, education, and other social areas. These advances are even more striking because they occurred during the 1980s, 1990s, and early 2000s—a time when the political climate of the United States was less inclined toward radical reform than in previous decades. This suggests that the basic concepts of sexual equality have become a mainstream value accepted by a large percentage of the American population.

This transition was neither immediate nor painless, however, and many people argue that it is not yet complete. For instance, even as more career opportunities have become available to women, they still face unfair treatment in the workplace, including inferior pay and a "glass ceiling" that prevents them from attaining the highest levels of executive power. The so-called "wage gap" between men and women remains in place today, with the median income of female workers about three-quarters that of males. Both inside and outside the workplace, personal attitudes and cultural biases continue to make a person's sex a basis for unfair treatment. Nonetheless, the environment that

The fourteen female senators of the 108th Congress pose for a group picture on Capitol Hill on January 9, 2003. In the front row, seated from left to right, are Olympia Snowe (R-Maine), Blanche Lincoln (D-Arkansas), Barbara Boxer (D-California), Susan Collins (R-Maine), Diane Feinstein (D-California), and Maria Cantwell (D-Washington). In the back row are Mary Landrieu (seated, D-Louisiana), Hillary Rodham Clinton (D-New York), Elizabeth Dole (R-North Carolina), Kay Bailey Hutchison (R-Texas), Barbara Mikulski (D-Maryland), Lisa Murkowski (R-Alaska), Debbie Stabenow (D-Michigan), and Patty Murray (D-Washington).

prevails in today's educational institutions and corporate headquarters is more respectful and appreciative of women and their abilities than ever before.

As women have assumed a more prominent role in American society, a host of other changes have come about—and some of them have created controversy. The resurgence of the women's rights movement in the 1960s and 1970s heightened the debate about a number of issues, including traditional gender roles in marriage and reproductive rights. As divisive as such topics have been, they help place women's suffrage in perspective. Today, it is impossible to imagine a debate about these and many other issues of national import without the active participation of women, whatever their political orientation. Their long years of wandering in the political wilderness have given way to a new era, one in which they play pivotal roles in shaping the political, economic, and cultural future of the nation.

BIOGRAPHIES

Susan B. Anthony (1820-1906)
Women's Suffrage Pioneer and President of the National American Woman Suffrage Association

Susan Brownell Anthony was born February 15, 1820, in Adams, Massachusetts, the second of seven children born to Daniel Anthony and Lucy (Read) Anthony. Susan's father initially worked as a farmer, but he became wealthy by starting a cotton mill, an enterprise in which his wife and children assisted. Despite their prosperity, the Anthonys lived a simple life in keeping with the tenants of their Quaker faith. The Quakers also believed in equality between the sexes, so Anthony grew up around outspoken women. This quality was not found in her quiet, inhibited mother, however. Lucy Anthony had been raised outside the Society of Friends, and she never joined because she felt she was "not good enough."

Anthony was educated in local schools and later at a home school started by her father. As a teenager, she spent her summers teaching younger children. At age seventeen, when Anthony was in her first year at a Philadelphia boarding school, her father's businesses failed in the financial panic of 1837. This blow to the family forced Anthony to give up her education and take a job as an assistant teacher in New Rochelle, New York. She taught school for the next ten years in a variety of New York towns but eventually grew bored with her work and began to look for other outlets. In her late twenties, she became increasingly drawn to the example of her father, whose views on slavery, alcohol, and other issues had made him a radical among his fellow Quakers. Proclaiming that "reform must be the watchword," Anthony formed a temperance group in the town where she was teaching.

In 1849 Anthony quit her job and rejoined her parents, who had moved to Rochester, New York. This brought Anthony into the thick of radical abolitionist activism, for her parents had made their farm a depot on the Underground Railroad and a favorite gathering place for such famous abolitionists as Frederick Douglass and William Lloyd Garrison. Susan joined in the spirit-

105

ed discussions that took place in the home, and it was during this time that she became intrigued by a new cause that had been launched a year earlier in nearby Seneca Falls—the fight for women's suffrage.

The Suffrage Soldier

After some initial reluctance, Anthony was won over to the new movement. She was unsure that she would be able to speak before large crowds—a prized skill for any social activist of the mid-1800s—but she developed what one journalist called "a capital voice."

Anthony's activism and outspoken nature soon made her a target. The *Utica Evening Herald,* for instance, called her "personally disgusting" and "a shrewish maiden" in an 1852 article. Critics also seized on Anthony's single marital status to depict her as a bitter spinster who had taken up suffrage when she could not find a husband. In truth, she had at least two marriage proposals and several other suitors but refused them all. "I never felt I could give up my life of freedom to become a man's housekeeper," she said. "[Marriage] would have meant dropping the work to which I had set my hand."

Anthony's sense of mission often made her impatient with suffrage leaders such as Elizabeth Cady Stanton and Lucy Stone who opted for marriage and family. In a letter to Stanton, she complained that "you … have all given yourselves over to *baby making,* & left poor brainless *me* to battle alone." For the most part, however, she did not let these feelings harm the cooperative relationship she and Stanton developed over the years. On a number of occasions, Anthony even ensconced herself at the Stanton household and took charge of the children so that their mother could concentrate on drafting an important speech.

For Anthony, this was all part of the work, and the work almost never stopped. She went from meeting to meeting, speech to speech, using her spare moments to plot strategy and fire off letters to her colleagues. This relentless pace continued for most of fifty years. Along the way she left mixed impressions. Her association with pro-suffrage racists like George Francis Train brought controversy, and her intensity and dedication sometimes led her to criticize fellow suffragists who could not match her zeal for the cause. But many colleagues recognized that Anthony's sharp tongue reflected the depth of her convictions. In 1865 Stanton wrote a letter that was typical of this attitude, telling Anthony that "your abuse is sweeter to me than anybody else's praise for, in spite of your severity, your faith and confidence shine through all."

One of Anthony's proudest endeavors was the launching of *The Revolution* in 1868. She believed that the paper was a much-needed way for women to "make our own claim in our own time." During the paper's two-year life span, she worked tirelessly to keep it afloat. When it failed, she was heartbroken. "I feel a great, calm sadness like that of a mother binding out a dear child that she could not support," Anthony said. Worse yet, she had to shoulder the entire $10,000 debt that remained after the paper folded. (Stanton, the paper's cofounder, was exempt from the debt and did not help to pay it.) "I sanguinely hope to cancel this debt in two years of hard work," Anthony said. It would take her six years, but she paid back the full amount.

This money was largely raised through Anthony's Lyceum lectures, which meant many more hard miles of traveling. Her speeches—whether for pay or on behalf of a suffrage campaign—took her to almost every area of the country, including the rugged states and territories of the Far West. When the train lines had yet to reach the town she sought, she sometimes slogged her way to meetings on stagecoaches, wagons, and even donkeys.

The Living Legend

In 1869 long-simmering philosophical differences erupted between various camps of the American Woman's Suffrage Movement (AWSA)—the leading suffrage organization of the era—leading Anthony and Stanton to found a more militant organization called the National Woman's Suffrage Association (NWSA). Stanton led the NWSA until 1890, when the AWSA and NWSA reunited to form the National American Woman's Suffrage Association (NAWSA).

In 1876 Stanton, Anthony, and Matilda Joslyn Gage began work on *History of Woman Suffrage,* a chronicle of the movement. It would eventually fill six large volumes (the final three put together by other editors). This type of collaboration between Stanton and Anthony became less common as Stanton withdrew from the suffrage movement in the following decades, but the two women remained on good terms.

By the late 1800s, Anthony's fame had surpassed that of her friend; in fact, she became a sort of living symbol of the women's suffrage movement in the final years of the nineteenth century. But the accolades had no impact on her famous work ethic. In 1894, for example, she visited all sixty counties in

New York over a three-month period to promote a suffrage referendum. Two years later, at age seventy-six, she spent eight months on the road in California. As she approached her eighties, she observed that "I should be just as well if I reached the end on the [railroad] cars or anywhere else as at home."

Anthony served as president of the NAWSA from 1892 to 1900, when she handed over the reins of leadership to Carrie Chapman Catt. After her retirement, she spent the majority of her time at the Rochester family home that she and her sister Mary had taken over in the early 1890s. She attended her final NAWSA convention in Baltimore in 1906, and at a birthday celebration in Washington, D.C., a few weeks later, she left her supporters with her final public declaration on the cause of suffrage: "failure is impossible!" Anthony contracted pneumonia during the trip, though, and upon her return to Rochester she was bedridden. As she lingered near death, she offered a sadder observation on the movement that had taken up the majority of her life. "I have been striving for over sixty years for a little bit of justice no bigger than that," she said, "and yet I must die without obtaining it. Oh, it seems so cruel!" She passed away on March 13, 1906.

Sources

Barry, Kathleen. *Susan B. Anthony: A Biography of a Singular Feminist.* New York: New York University Press, 1988.

Gurko, Miriam. *The Ladies of Seneca Falls: The Birth of the Woman's Rights Movement.* New York: Macmillan, 1974.

Sherr, Lynn. *Susan B. Anthony: In Her Own Words.* New York: Times Books, 1995.

Ward, Geoffrey C. *Not For Ourselves Alone: The Story of Elizabeth Cady Stanton and Susan B. Anthony.* New York: Knopf, 1999.

Carrie Chapman Catt (1859-1947)
President of the National American Woman Suffrage Association

Born Carrie Clinton Lane on February 9, 1859, in Ripon, Wisconsin, Catt was the second of three children born to Maria (Clinton) Lane and Lucius Lane, who ran their own farm. Catt's father had previously been a gold prospector in California and was known for his stubborn personality and hard work. Her mother had attended college (then a rare accomplishment for a woman), where she had been influenced by feminist thought. When Catt was seven the family relocated to a farm near Charles City, Iowa. Catt's inquisitive intelligence showed itself early on, and after completing high school, she decided to attend the newly opened Iowa State Agricultural College (now Iowa State University). Though her father harbored doubts about the need for any woman to have a college education, he gave his daughter $25 per year toward her room and board. Catt earned the rest of the money she needed by teaching school. While at the university, Catt sought and won new opportunities for female students, including the right to deliver speeches before the literary society. She promptly used that right make a speech on behalf of women's suffrage. When she received her degree in science in 1880, she was the only female in her graduating class.

Catt became a high school teacher in Mason City, Iowa, soon advancing to the position of superintendent for all of the town's schools. She gave up her education career for marriage, wedding Leo Chapman, a journalist and ardent suffragist, in 1885. Their time together was short: Chapman contracted typhoid fever the following year while visiting California. By the time Catt arrived in San Francisco, her husband was dead.

Catt remained in San Francisco and supported herself by working as a journalist and public speaker. During this period she developed the commanding stage presence and thundering voice that would serve her well in the decades to come. Though suffrage was still important to her, most of her speeches focused on her conviction that the masses of foreigners arriving in the United States during that era were undermining American values—a view she would later renounce.

In 1887 Catt returned to Iowa where, in addition to continuing her speaking career, she devoted time to the causes of temperance and women's suffrage. In 1890, following her marriage to George Catt, a well-paid engineer, she was able to devote all of her energies to women's voting rights. "He was as much a reformer as I," Catt said of her husband. "What he could do was to earn a living enough for two … and thus I could reform for two." After joining the National American Woman Suffrage Association (NAWSA), Catt made a positive impression on Susan B. Anthony and other suffrage leaders during the failed South Dakota suffrage campaign of 1890. Two years later she was appointed the head of NAWSA's business committee.

In 1893 Catt agreed to campaign on behalf of Colorado's suffrage referendum after other NAWSA officials refused to aid the state's activists. "Remember I am not coming to be *bossy* but only to help," she wrote to the head of Colorado suffragists. Her help included detailed directives on how to organize the precincts, and two months of lectures and speeches from one end of the state to the other. When the referendum won by a large margin, Catt became one of the rising stars of the suffrage movement. She cemented her reputation by overseeing a second win for pro-suffrage forces in Idaho in 1896 and by founding NAWSA's Organization Committee, which vastly improved the association's methods of creating and educating local chapters.

Becomes President of NAWSA

In 1900 Susan B. Anthony named Catt as her successor as president of the NAWSA. During her first tenure as president, Catt stepped up efforts to modernize the organization and, most importantly, to grow its membership and treasury. She also began her entry into international affairs by helping found the International Woman Suffrage Alliance (IWSA) in 1902. All of Catt's work came to a stop in 1904, however, after her husband was beset by serious health problems. His death the following year from a perforated ulcer was a serious blow to Catt. Her own health lapsed, and she withdrew from activism for many months.

When she returned to action, Catt devoted much of her energy to the IWSA. Working as a global ambassador for the suffrage cause, she spent a lot of time in Europe and completed an around-the-world voyage in the early 1910s, with extended stops in South Africa, India, and China. Her travels gave her a new perspective on the world. "Once I was a regular jingo," she said, "but that was before I visited other countries. I had thought America had a monopoly on all that stands for progress, but I had a sad awakening." Catt's internationalism was a factor in her decision to help found the Woman's Peace Party after the beginning of World War I, but she did not take a large role in the organization, and within a few years both she and NAWSA threw their official support behind the U.S. war effort.

When Anna Howard Shaw resigned as president of NAWSA in December 1915, Catt was pressured to take the job. She did not welcome the idea, but she finally relented. "It will kill me," she said, "but I will do it." Despite her reservations, Catt immediately went to work. In the ensuing months she unveiled her "Winning Plan," a new political strategy that proved instrumental in securing passage of the Nineteenth Amendment.

Even before final ratification of the Nineteenth Amendment, Catt was transforming NAWSA into the National League of Women Voters (NLWV). In describing the new group, Catt said that it would be dedicated to "the education of women citizens, piloting them through the first years of political participation." The NLWV also set out to "support improved legislation" but refrained from promoting particular candidates or parties.

Peace Advocate

With the suffrage fight over, Catt again turned her attention to international affairs. She resumed her activities with the IWSA, but increasingly focused on the larger issues of war and peace. Following the end of World War I, she believed that women could play a key role in avoiding future bloodshed. In 1921 she told the NLWV convention that "the people in this room tonight could put an end to war" and proclaimed that "God is calling to the women of the world to come forward and stay the hands of men." In 1925 she formed the Committee on the Cause and Cure for War. The group held annual conferences up until 1939, when it became clear that if there was a cure, it was not going to arrive in time to prevent World War II.

During World War II, Catt helped publicize the atrocities committed against the Jews and served as an advocate for Jewish refugees. By this point, her years of global travel were behind her, and she spent most of her time in her home in New Rochelle, New York. She died there of a heart attack on March 9, 1947, at the age of eighty-eight.

Sources

Adams, Mildred. *The Right to Be People.* Philadelphia: Lippincott, 1967.

Graham, Sara Hunter. *Woman Suffrage and the New Democracy.* New Haven, CT: Yale University Press, 1996.

Van Voris, Jacqueline. *Carrie Chapman Catt: A Public Life.* New York: Feminist Press at the City University of New York, 1987.

Laura Clay (1849-1941)
Promoter of State-based Suffrage and Opponent of the Nineteenth Amendment

Laura Clay was born February 9, 1849, near Richmond, Kentucky. She was the daughter of Mary Jane (Warfield) Clay and Cassius Marcellus Clay. At the time of her birth, her father was already well known. A hero of the Mexican-American War, he also was one of the few prominent abolitionists in the South. (His fame extended into the twentieth century, when he served as the namesake for the boxer who later became Muhammad Ali.) At the outset of the Civil War, Cassius Clay became U.S. ambassador to Russia, so when Laura was twelve years old, she spent several months in Moscow before returning to Kentucky. Because her father was frequently absent, Laura's mother was the primary manager of the large estate where the family lived. During the Civil War, Mary Jane Clay offered aid to the Union Army, and Confederate troops raided the farm on one occasion and burned several buildings.

Laura was educated at Sayre Female Institute in Lexington, graduating in 1865, then attended a finishing school in New York City for a year. Soon thereafter Clay's life was affected by the marital problems of her parents. Her father returned from Russia in 1869—and so did a four-year-old boy that Cassius Clay had fathered while abroad. Laura's parents soon separated, and they divorced in 1878. Due to the inequality of the marriage laws, her mother was deprived of any share in the estate she had run for almost a decade. In her diary, Clay wrote that this incident taught her "the unjust relations between men and women," and she vowed that "the great cause of Woman's Rights" was to be her life's work.

That work was rather slow in starting. Clay attended the University of Michigan for a year, then devoted herself to running her own farm, which she had inherited from her father. Finally, as Clay approached her fortieth birthday in the late 1880s, she made women's rights a priority, founding the Kentucky Equal Rights Association. In 1894 Clay and her colleagues scored their first major victory by convincing the Kentucky legislature to pass a new property-rights law that gave married women more control over real estate holdings and personal property.

Voice of the South

By the mid-1890s Clay had emerged as one of the most prominent suffragists in the southern United States. This region had made little progress in extending voting rights to women, partially because it tended to have conservative views about the role of females and partially because of its legacy of slavery and troubled race relations. In pursuing the vote for women, Clay, like many other Southern suffragists, tried to turn the race issue into an asset. She argued that only women who could read and write should be granted the right to vote. Since more white women met this criteria than blacks, this arrangement would help ensure that white Southerners continued to hold political and economic dominion over African Americans.

At first glance, Clay's perspective seems distant from the ideas of her abolitionist father. But in reality, their views were not that different. Cassius Clay believed that slavery was wrong, but he did not pursue total racial equality. Similarly, Laura Clay was active in aiding the black community in various ways, but she did not believe that African Americans as a whole were prepared to take an equal role in politics.

Nonetheless, Clay's attitudes were relatively progressive for her time and place. Some of her colleagues felt that blacks, educated or not, should be permanently barred from voting under all circumstances. Clay rejected these ideas and instead envisioned a South where African Americans would one day assume a fuller social and political role—once they had mastered the nuances of the nation's political and cultural structure and proven themselves worthy of full participation in that structure. She genuinely believed that her literacy plan for female suffrage was a progressive measure that would help bring increased opportunities for blacks. But, as Paul E. Fuller writes in *Laura Clay and the Woman's Rights Movement*, her paternalistic attitudes also "provided a convenient excuse for the worst sort of discrimination."

Southern suffragists such as Clay and Kate Gordon of Louisiana saw their prominence grow in the 1890s and the first decade of the 1900s. They helped to steer the National American Woman Suffrage Association (NAWSA) toward pursuing suffrage on the state rather than the national level and also convinced

NAWSA to affirm the concept of states' rights. These were important steps for the Southerners because they were opposed to passage of a federal constitutional amendment that would weaken the power of the states and would likely give the vote to all women, ignoring questions of education and race. Clay was influential in several other ways, as well. She served on NAWSA's business committee between 1896 and 1911 and was appointed chair of NAWSA's Increase of Membership Committee in 1902, where she helped pioneer new strategies to expand the association's membership rolls and improve its finances.

A Suffragist against Suffrage

The 1910s did not prove kind to the fortunes of Southern suffragists such as Clay. By 1916 both NAWSA and the National Woman's Party were pushing for the federal amendment and placing less emphasis on state measures. Clay adopted a neutral position on these efforts. Overall, she did not believe that the federal amendment had much chance for success, but in this she was wrong. As the Nineteenth Amendment made its way through Congress in 1919, she faced a difficult choice: should she endorse the amendment, knowing it would finally give women the vote, or oppose it because it violated the concept of states' rights to which she had always been allegiant? In the end, Clay decided to oppose the Nineteenth Amendment. She even joined Kate Gordon in Nashville in the summer of 1920 as part of an organized effort to keep Tennessee from becoming the thirty-sixth state to ratify the amendment.

When this battle was lost, Clay accepted the outcome and moved on. She became active not only as a voter but also as a politician. She participated in the Kentucky Democratic Party and made a failed bid for a seat in the state senate in 1923. Despite her opposition to the Nineteenth Amendment, she remained on good terms with most of her old women's rights allies and was a respected figure among younger female activists. When Kentucky ratified the Nineteenth Amendment, one Kentucky suffragist noted that "it is only proper that recognition should be given to Miss Laura Clay, who for a quarter of a century when the cause of woman suffrage seemed but an incandescent dream, labored, toiled, spoke, spent herself and her wealth to advance that cause." Clay died in her Kentucky home on June 29, 1941.

Sources

Fuller, Paul E. *Laura Clay and the Woman's Rights Movement.* Lexington, KY: The University Press of Kentucky, 1975.

Weatherford, Doris. *A History of the American Suffragist Movement.* Santa Barbara, CA: ABC-CLIO, 1998.

Abigail Scott Duniway (1834-1915)
Women's Suffrage Activist in the Pacific Northwest

Born Abigail Jane Scott on October 22, 1834, in Tazewell County, Illinois, Duniway was the third of twelve children raised by Ann (Roelofson) Scott and John Tucker Scott. Hers was a hardworking farm family, and her parents expected their children to pitch in as soon as they were able. She milked cows, planted corn, made butter, and at age nine resodded the family's lawn. This final task took such a severe physical toll on Duniway that she later blamed it for a "chronic weakness of the spine" that afflicted her for the rest of her life.

In 1852 the Scott family pulled up stakes and set out for Oregon. An aspiring writer, seventeen-year-old Abigail was charged with keeping a journal of the wagon trip west. She dutifully recorded their experiences throughout the journey west, including the tragic deaths of her mother—who had opposed the trip—and her youngest brother on the way. The rest of the family settled in Lafayette, a small town in northwestern Oregon where Abigail found employment as a teacher.

In 1853 Abigail married Benjamin Charles Duniway. They established a farm and had six children over the next nine years. Duniway disliked farm work, describing it as "general pioneer drudge," but she managed to find time to develop her writing skills while working at her other chores. In 1859 she published her first book, *Captain Gray's Company,* which was based on her family's trip west. Several other books, both poetry and novels, would follow over the course of her life. Duniway also became a regular contributor to the *Oregon Farmer.* Her column highlighted the difficulties faced by female settlers and represented her first public declarations of support for greater women's rights.

These sentiments reflected the influence of Horace Greeley's *New York Tribune,* a progressive paper that Duniway had long enjoyed, as well as the example of her father, a low-key but steady supporter of temperance, abolition, and other societal reforms. Most of all, though, Duniway's ideas were based on her own difficult experiences as a working wife.

Spreading the Word

More difficulties were just ahead. The Duniways lost their farm in 1862 when they defaulted on a loan. Soon after, Benjamin Duniway suffered injuries in a wagon accident that left him unable to do heavy work. Forced to support the family herself, Duniway opened a boarding school in Lafayette. Three years later she moved the school to the larger town of Albany and also opened a shop selling hats and other goods. Her store prospered and became a place where women talked over their problems. These discussions convinced Duniway that women desperately needed the vote to improve their circumstances.

Duniway threw herself into the suffrage struggle with typical determination. She founded the State Equal Suffrage Society in 1870 and moved her family to Portland the following year. Soon after relocating, she launched a women's rights paper, *New Northwest*. She convinced Susan B. Anthony to visit Oregon in 1871, and the two women conducted an extensive tour of the Pacific Northwest. Soon after, Duniway became an energetic member of Anthony's National Woman's Suffrage Association (NWSA) and eventually became a vice president in the association.

Duniway's campaigning for women's suffrage frequently took her to neighboring Washington, then still a territory. It was there that she got her first taste of success, as the territorial legislature gave women the vote in 1883. Her influence was also felt in Idaho, where she was a part-time resident between 1887 and 1894. Duniway helped ignite the state's suffrage movement, and in 1896, Idaho's women won the vote.

As Duniway became better known she also became more controversial. Some observers criticized her as hot-tempered and egotistical, but most of the condemnation she received stemmed from her unconventional views on various issues. Religion was one point of contention, with Duniway frequently criticizing what she called the "puffed up churchanity of the nineteenth century" and clashing with religious figures that she saw as overly pious and hypocritical. Her views on alcohol were even more divisive. Unlike many suffrage advocates, Duniway did not favor laws that prohibited beer, wine, and liquor. She felt that such legal measures represented "intolerance and quackery" and would prove unworkable. Further, Duniway believed that the cause of women's suffrage was being harmed because of its links to the anti-alcohol crusade. With this in mind, she became an advocate of the "still-hunt" method of pursuing the vote, in which suffragists lobbied legislators in a persistent but low-key manner so as to avoid rousing the opposition of powerful alcohol interests.

A Final Win

Duniway remained a key player in the suffrage movement into the early 1900s. Her efforts helped put women's suffrage referenda on the Oregon ballot in 1900, 1906, 1908, and 1910. All of these proposals failed, however, and the 1906 loss was especially bitter. The National American Woman Suffrage Association (NAWSA) played a large role in that campaign, which was rocked when NAWSA president Anna Howard Shaw maneuvered to replace Duniway at the helm of the campaign effort. Duniway was forced to resign, and she could only watch from the sidelines as Shaw and her cohorts enlisted the assistance of the Women's Christian Temperance Union in the campaign. As Duniway predicted, this development mobilized the liquor interests against the referendum. Their opposition proved pivotal in turning Oregon voters against the measure. This turn of events soured relations between Duniway and the NAWSA leaders for many years. She received no assistance from the national organization for either the 1908 or 1910 campaigns, both of which failed.

Yet another referendum was placed on the ballot for 1912. Its chances for passage looked promising because several other western states had recently given women the vote, but Duniway began that year bedeviled by pneumonia and blood poisoning. There was concern that she would not live until the election, but Duniway survived. Her fortitude served as an inspiration to other Oregon suffragists, and the referendum passed by a small margin. After more than forty years of effort, Duniway's vision for Oregon women had finally been realized. In the next election, she was given the honor of being the first woman in Oregon to cast a legal ballot in the state. She served as an advisor to other suffragists until her death on October 11, 1915.

Sources

Morrison, Dorothy Nafus. *Ladies Were Not Expected: Abigail Scott Duniway and Women's Rights.* New York: Atheneum, 1977.

Moynihan, Ruth Barnes. *Rebel for Rights: Abigail Scott Duniway.* New Haven, CT: Yale University Press, 1983.

Weatherford, Doris. *A History of the American Suffragist Movement.* Santa Barbara, CA: ABC-CLIO, 1998.

Lucretia Coffin Mott (1793-1880)
Religious Leader, Abolitionist, and Women's Suffrage Pioneer

Lucretia Mott

Lucretia Coffin was born on January 3, 1793, the daughter of Anna (Folger) Coffin and Thomas Coffin. She was part of a long line of Quakers born and raised on the island of Nantucket, off the coast of Massachusetts. At the time of Lucretia's birth, her father earned his living from whaling. This kept him away from home for extended periods, requiring Mott's mother to take an active role in organizing the family's affairs. Anna Coffin also operated her own shop, which gave Lucretia early lessons in how a woman could succeed at business functions that were normally handled by men.

After a harrowing three-year absence from his family on a whaling expedition, Mott's father opted to become a merchant. The family moved to Boston when Lucretia was eleven, and she attended public school there for two years. She then entered a boarding school run by the Society of Friends near Poughkeepsie, New York. In her late teens she rejoined her family, which had relocated to Philadelphia. In 1811 she married James Mott, with whom she would eventually have six children. They would remain Philadelphia residents for most of the rest of their lives.

Preaching and Reform

Mott began working as a teacher in Quaker schools in 1817. Around this same period, the death of her second child sparked a deepening of her religious beliefs and devotion to her faith. In 1821 she was formally recognized as a minister in the Society of Friends. Always outgoing and talkative, Mott developed a reputation for eloquent and well-reasoned sermons, and also for promoting progressive views on various societal issues. In 1827 she and her husband aligned themselves with the "Hicksite" faction of the Society of Friends, which promoted equality and democracy among members.

While the Hicksites represented the more liberal wing of Quakerism, the Motts were liberal even by Hicksite standards. This was especially true in regard to the issue of slavery. In the late 1820s and early 1830s, Mott and her husband became involved in the fledgling abolition movement, lending their support to noted abolitionist William Lloyd Garrison. In 1833 both James and Lucretia were present at the Philadelphia convention where the American Anti-slavery Society was formed. Initially the society barred women from joining, so Mott formed the Philadelphia Female Anti-Slavery Society, which included both black and white women. To protest slavery, the Motts refused to use or sell goods created by slave labor. In later years their home served as a stop on the Underground Railroad.

Mott's growing penchant for making abolitionist statements in her sermons led some Quaker meeting houses to distance themselves from her. When Mott and other women took their abolitionist message to the public at large, the reaction could be even more severe. Crowds of protestors gathered outside the Anti-Slavery Convention of American Women that was held in Philadelphia in 1838. Mott told the mixed audience of black and white delegates not to be put off "by a little appearance of danger," but subsequent events proved that she underestimated the peril they were in. On the fourth day of the convention, a mob of protestors stormed the hall and burned it to the ground (no delegates were caught in the blaze). Another angry mob threatened the activist in her home the very next day. "I was scarcely breathing," Mott recalled of the moment when the group approached her door, "but I felt willing to suffer whatever the cause required." At the last moment a neighbor averted the attack.

Embracing Women's Rights

Though slavery was Mott's primary cause in the 1830s, she also became increasingly interested in the subject of women's rights during this time. She was heavily influenced by Mary Wollstonecraft's *A Vindication of the Rights of Women,* which she called her "pet book." She also was familiar with the writings of the Grimké sisters, whom she knew personally.

In 1840 the topics of slavery and women's rights came together at the World Anti-Slavery Conference in London. When Mott, Elizabeth Cady Stanton, and other women were excluded from participating, they vowed to hold a women's rights convention in the United States. In the years following the London conference, Mott began to include references to the treatment of women in her public addresses, and over time she came to believe that equality between the sexes was "the most important question of my life." When the Seneca Falls Woman's Rights Convention finally took place in 1848, Mott's involvement was essential. In addition to being one of the primary organizers, the inclusion of her well-known name in the meeting notice helped draw a sizable crowd. Her self-assured familiarity in speaking before an audience kept the meeting on track and gave the other women courage. James Mott did his part by serving as chairperson of the two-day meeting.

In the years that followed, Mott's stature and abilities as an orator continued to aid the women's rights movement. Her most influential commentary on feminism took place in 1849. Responding to comments made by writer Richard Henry Dana that women were "physically, mentally, and morally weaker than men," Mott delivered her "Discourse on Woman." In it, she attacked the biblical justifications for the inferiority of the female sex and called for a more equitable form of marriage. Because she was still heavily involved in the fight against slavery, Mott tried to leave the responsibility for women's-rights organizing to others. This eventually came to pass, but she was often asked to preside at important early meetings of the women's rights movement, such as the national conventions of 1850, 1852, and 1853.

After the Civil War, Mott, then in her seventies, took a less active role in public affairs. Still, she agreed to serve as president of the American Equal Rights Association in 1866, the short-lived group that tried to promote the rights of both women and African Americans. Dismayed by the division in the suffrage movement that occurred in 1869, Mott tried to reunite the two groups but had little success. Her final involvement with the movement took place in 1878, when she attended ceremonies honoring the thirtieth anniversary of the Seneca Falls convention. There, Mott delivered a succinct summary of her views on women's rights: "give women the privilege of cooperating in making the laws, and there will be harmony without severity, justice without oppression." She died in her sleep a little more than two years later, on November 11, 1880.

Sources

Bryant, Jennifer Fisher. *Lucretia Mott: A Guiding Light.* Grand Rapids, MI: Eerdmans, 1996.

Gurko, Miriam. *The Ladies of Seneca Falls: The Birth of the Woman's Rights Movement.* New York: Macmillan, 1974.

Alice Paul (1885-1977)
Founder and President of the National Woman's Party

Alice Paul was born January 11, 1885, in Moorestown, New Jersey. She was the oldest of four children born to William Mickle Paul, a bank president, and Tacie (Parry) Paul. Her family belonged to the Society of Friends, and the Quaker traits of equality and public service were touchstones that guided Paul throughout her life. She once commented that "Quakers have always believed in Woman Suffrage," and her mother took Alice to suffrage meetings when she was still a child.

Paul entered Swarthmore College at age sixteen, and her performance in the political and economic curricula earned her a fellowship to the New York School of Philanthropy upon completion of her undergraduate studies. In 1907 she completed a master's degree in sociology at the University of Pennsylvania and that same year she went to study in England on another fellowship.

Though her studies in Britain were related to social work, Paul rapidly lost interest in the field. "I could see that social workers were not doing much good in the world," she said. Instead, she became a "heart and soul convert" to the Women's Social and Political Union (WSPU), the most radical of the groups pushing for women's suffrage in Great Britain. Led by Emmeline Pankhurst, the WSPU specialized in staging disruptive demonstrations in which its members were arrested. Once jailed, the demonstrators engaged in hunger strikes to protest their treatment.

Beginning in 1909, Paul took part in these activities. At one point she was charged with "assaulting two constables ... by striking them on the face with her hand." During one of her stints in jail Paul met Lucy Burns, an American of Irish descent who had recently joined the WSPU. The two became good friends and teamed up for several later demonstrations orchestrated by Pankhurst. Paul's experiences in Britain introduced her to militant protest, and they also deepened her anger at the treatment women received.

"To me it was shocking that a government of men could look with such extreme contempt on a movement that was asking nothing except such a simple little thing as the right to vote," she recalled.

Taking the Fight to Washington

Paul returned to the United States in 1910, underweight and suffering lingering health problems stemming from her experiences as a hunger striker. She spent two years earning her Ph.D. at the University of Pennsylvania, then turned her full attention to the American suffrage campaign. In 1912, with the support of Jane Addams, Paul convinced NAWSA leaders that she should head up the group's lobbying efforts in Washington, D.C., which had been neglected for many years. The group of activists that Paul put together to aid her in this mission grew into the Congressional Union and, eventually, the National Woman's Party. The first member of Paul's team was Lucy Burns, who had returned to America in 1912. "They are both political-minded," a colleague said of Paul and Burns. "They seemed in those early days to have one spirit and one brain."

Though individuals such as Burns, Anne Martin, Crystal Eastman, and Elsie Hill proved essential additions to the National Woman's Party (NWP), Paul remained the undisputed leader despite her relative youth. Paul's authority came from a combination of quiet intensity, keen intelligence, and inexhaustible energy. "She has in the first place a devotion to the cause which is absolutely self-sacrificing," said Maud Younger, another of Paul's assistants. "She recognizes no obstacles. She has a clear, penetrating, analytic mind that which cleaves straight to the heart of things." Paul's actions in Washington even surprised Lucy Burns, who had known her previously. "I was staggered by her speed and industry," Burns said, "and the way she could raise money."

Paul's dedication to the suffrage movement allowed little time for socializing, so she sometimes appeared cold and brusque. Others criticized her as being too powerful, but these complaints usually came from those outside the organization. Most colleagues backed their leader whole-heartedly and tried to match her devotion to the cause. Together, their efforts brought about the militant protests that played an essential part in the passage of the Nineteenth Amendment.

Pursuing Equal Rights

After women's suffrage was won, Paul helped steer the NWP toward a new goal—passage of the Equal Rights Amendment (ERA), which she drafted in 1923. She continued to push for its passage for the rest of her life, though with little success. The amendment's difficulties were partly caused by its controversial insistence on gender equality and partly because the NWP and the women's rights movement as a whole lost steam in the 1920s. Paul later commented that "everybody went back to their respective homes" after the Nineteenth Amendment was passed. This was certainly true of Lucy Burns, who declared that "I am not going to fight … any more" and settled into a quieter life. Many others did the same or found different political battles to fight. Paul's devotion to women's rights, however, never flagged.

Convinced that a solid understanding of the legal code would help her efforts, Paul earned three law degrees in the 1920s. In the 1930s she helped found the World Party for Equal Rights for Women (also known as the World Woman's Party), which took her to Geneva, Switzerland, in the late 1930s and early 1940s. Following World War II she helped secure the inclusion of gender-equality principles in the United Nations Charter and promoted the establishment of the U.N. Commission on the Status of Women.

In the 1940s Paul faced growing opposition from within the NWP, as some party members charged that she had become too autocratic. These struggles left her with less power, but she was still an important player. She helped shape the Civil Rights Act of 1964 so that it included references to sex discrimination and was successful in getting other women's groups to support the ERA. With the resurgence of the women's rights movement in the 1960s and 1970s, Paul had the satisfaction of seeing the amendment passed by Congress in 1972. At the time of her death she had high expectations that the ERA would be ratified by the necessary number of states, but that failed to occur.

Like her hero Susan B. Anthony, Paul never married. She lived with her sister Helen for many years and later with fellow activist Elsie Hill. Following Hill's death in the late 1960s, Paul lived in nursing homes in Ridgefield, Connecticut, and Moorestown, New Jersey—the city where she was born. She died of heart failure on July 9, 1977, at age ninety-two.

Sources

Ford, Linda G. *Iron-Jawed Angels: The Suffrage Militancy of the National Woman's Party, 1912-1920.* Lanham, MD: University Press of America, 1991.

Irwin, Inez Hayes. *The Story of Alice Paul and the National Woman's Party.* Fairfax, VA: Denlinger's, 1977.

Lunardini, Christine A. *From Equal Suffrage to Equal Rights: Alice Paul and the National Woman's Party, 1910-1928.* New York: New York University Press, 1986.

Elizabeth Cady Stanton (1815-1902)
Women's Suffrage Pioneer and President of the National Woman's Suffrage Association and the National American Woman Suffrage Association

Elizabeth Cady Stanton was born on November 12, 1815, in Johnstown, New York, the daughter of Daniel Cady and Margaret (Livingston) Cady. Her family was very affluent, partly due to the wealth her mother had inherited and partly from the shrewd real estate investments made by her father. Daniel Cady had also distinguished himself as a lawyer, judge, and politician, serving in Congress and as an associate justice of the New York Supreme Court.

Stanton was schooled at Johnstown Academy and then at the Troy Female Seminary in Troy, New York, where she graduated in 1833. Possessed with a keen intelligence and a dislike for the rules set down by her parents and teachers, Stanton's rebellious streak was visible throughout her childhood. "I am so tired of that everlasting no! no! no!," she said. "At school, at home, everywhere it is a *no!*" She found herself drawn to other rebels. Gerrit Smith, her mother's cousin, was involved in most of the reform efforts of the mid-1800s, including abolition and temperance, and Stanton came to cherish the weeks she spent at Smith's estate each summer. There, Stanton said, she "felt a new inspiration in life and was enthused with new ideas of individual rights."

During a visit to Smith's home in 1839, she met Henry Stanton, an abolitionist employed by the American Anti-Slavery Society. The two were married in 1840. As part of their honeymoon they attended the World Anti-Slavery Conference in London, but Elizabeth and other abolitionist women, including Lucretia Mott, were prohibited from taking part in the discussions. Angry at their treatment, Stanton and Mott made vague plans to hold a women's rights convention when they returned in the United States. But these plans did not come to fruition for several years.

The Stantons settled in Boston in 1845, where their first three children were born. Elizabeth enjoyed big-city life, but when her husband's law practice faltered, the family relocated to Seneca Falls, New York, in 1847. Elizabeth Stanton immediately became dissatisfied with her new life. There was little intellectual stimulation in the small town, and she was forced to take on more of the household duties herself.

When Stanton was reunited with Lucretia Mott the following year, they fell into an earnest discussion of her disenchantment with married life. "I poured out ... the torrent of my long accumulating discontent, with such vehemence and indignation that I stirred myself as well as the rest of the party to do and dare anything," Stanton recalled. Indeed, this conversation breathed new life into the embers of discontent that had been created seven years before at the anti-slavery conference in London. The two women quickly agreed that the time had come to make their vision of a woman's rights convention become a reality.

Housewife and Revolutionary

Even after Stanton and Mott helped organize the historic Seneca Falls Convention of 1848—commonly recognized as the birthplace of the women's suffrage movement in the United States—the domestic conditions of her life did not change dramatically. She continued to have children, eventually giving birth to five sons and two daughters. Her parental obligations meant that Stanton's contributions to the movement centered more on writing, theorizing, and plotting strategy than on prolonged campaigning. Fortunately, her ability to craft ideas and put them into words were her strongest gifts. Her ability to explain the desire of women for more equitable treatment—and describe the societal benefits that would accrue from such changes—made her an invaluable member of the movement.

Stanton's growing fame did not set well with Judge Cady, who criticized his daughter's activism. Stanton also felt some resistance from her husband, who was sometimes put off by her outspokenness and may have been jealous of the attention she received. For her part, Stanton resented the fact that Henry was frequently away from home pursuing his political and business career while she was left to handle the children on her own. She accompanied Henry to New York City during the Civil War when he received a position as a customs official, but their relationship remained stormy. From the late 1860s forward they largely lived apart, though they never divorced.

The lack of family support did not deter Stanton to any great degree. She remained a staunch voice for suffrage, and she regularly criticized the inequities in marriage relations and American divorce laws. Stanton's statements on these issues caused discord within the women's rights movement, but Stanton remained convinced that "this marriage question ... lies at the very foundation of all progress." The years following the Civil War were Stanton's most active, as she became embroiled in the movement's internal debates over the Fourteenth and Fifteenth Amendments. Her alliance during this period with pro-suffrage racists like businessman George Francis Train appalled many fellow activists, but she refused to disassociate herself from anyone who she viewed as an asset in the suffrage cause.

When Stanton's efforts to secure women's voting rights in this era failed, she became somewhat disillusioned. She seemed to sum up her feelings many years later when she wrote that "our enfranchisement ought to have occurred in Reconstruction days.... Our movement is belated and like all things too long postponed now gets on everybody's nerves."

In the 1870s a lot of Stanton's time was taken up with public speaking tours. While these lectures were valuable in promoting the general message of women's equality, they kept her away from other lobbying efforts. In the 1880s she withdrew from the battlefield even more, leaving the United States and spending extended periods in Europe. Some historians have attributed her disengagement to her restless and inquisitive mind. "I cannot work in the same old ruts any longer," she declared at one point. "I have said all I have to say on the subject of suffrage." Instead, she began devoting more attention to the subject of religion. This interest culminated in 1895 with *The Woman's Bible,* a critique of commonly held religious beliefs that triggered rebukes from a wide array of American religious leaders and criticism from fellow women's rights activists as well.

Stanton's health problems mounted in her final years. She put on a lot of weight, had difficulty walking, and lost most of her eyesight. Her final address to the National American Woman Suffrage Association in 1895 had to be read by someone else because she found it too difficult to stand at the podium. Her mind remained active to the end, however. She regularly published newspaper and magazine articles in the final years of her life, and on the day before she died she composed a letter to President Theodore Roosevelt calling on him to bring about "the complete emancipation of thirty-six million women." She died on October 26, 1902, in her New York City apartment.

Sources

Banner, Lois W. *Elizabeth Cady Stanton: A Radical for Woman's Rights.* Boston: Little, Brown, 1980.

Goldsmith, Barbara. *Other Powers: The Age of Suffrage, Spiritualism, and the Scandalous Victoria Woodhull.* New York: Knopf, 1998.

Gurko, Miriam. *The Ladies of Seneca Falls: The Birth of the Woman's Rights Movement.* New York: Macmillan, 1974.

Ward, Geoffrey C. *Not for Ourselves Alone: The Story of Elizabeth Cady Stanton and Susan B. Anthony.* New York: Knopf, 1999.

Lucy Stone (1818-1893)
Women's Suffrage Pioneer and Founder of the American Woman Suffrage Association

Born August 13, 1818, near West Brookfield, Massachusetts, Stone was the sixth of seven surviving children born to Hannah (Matthews) Stone and Francis Stone, who were farmers. Her parents were very traditional when it came to family leadership and decision making. "There was only one will in our family, and that was my father's," Stone later explained. But Lucy began asserting herself at a young age despite her father's opposition. After completing her primary education at age fourteen, she announced her desire to continue in school, as her older brothers had done. Her father was astonished at this proposition and refused to give or lend Lucy any tuition funds. Stone was undaunted, and at age sixteen she began teaching in area schools and saving as much money as possible. She was able to pursue her studies sporadically at several different institutions in Massachusetts over the next nine years. During this time, Stone began participating in antislavery activities and was influenced by abolitionists William Lloyd Garrison and Abby Kelly (later Abby Kelly Foster).

In 1843 Stone entered Oberlin College in Oberlin, Ohio, the first institution of higher learning in the country to accept female students. While Oberlin was a center for reformers of various sorts, Stone's emphasis on better treatment for women broke new ground at the college. Classmate and close friend Antoinette Brown (later Antoinette Brown Blackwell) said that Stone was considered "a rather dangerous person" at Oberlin. Stone challenged the college's rules against women speaking in public and staged a successful one-person strike so that female teachers in the college's preparatory academy would be paid as much as the men. This raise in pay—along with some grudgingly dispensed financial assistance from her father—allowed Stone to eke out a frugal existence at the school. She earned a bachelor of arts degree in 1847.

Convinced that her life must be used "to promote the highest good in the world," Stone decided to become a public lecturer. Though women's rights were her foremost concern, she began as a speaker for the Massachusetts Anti-Slavery Society in 1848. This proved to be a difficult profession, especially given widespread societal disapproval of women who spoke in public. Pro-slavery figures sometimes infiltrated the audience to heckle Stone and other speakers or pelt them with fruit and other materials. On occasion, riots of an even more violent nature broke out. Stone, however, developed a reputation as a patient and confident speaker, even in the face of abuse. "Her manner was ... gentle, calm, dignified, earnest," wrote a reporter from the *Pennsylvania Freeman* in 1848. "She spoke ... with a quiet self-possession that was perfectly charming." Stone used common language and punctuated her talks with interesting stories. But her most formidable tool was her clear, musical speaking voice.

Stone soon began speaking about women's equality in addition to abolition. In 1851 she made women's rights her top priority, although she remained active in the Massachusetts Anti-Slavery Society. Her efforts to spread the message of women's rights were all the more impressive because there was no formal organization to back her in the early years. She was responsible for all travel and booking arrangements and bore the responsibility for the financial success or failure of her engagements. In addition, Stone was instrumental in arranging the national woman's rights conventions that took place throughout the 1850s, working alongside Lucretia Mott, Susan B. Anthony, and other leaders of the movement.

Union and Discord

Stone had vowed not to marry at an early age, and she was ardently opposed to the existing marriage laws that gave favorable treatment to men. Several suitors tried to make her change her mind, but Stone resisted them, once saying "'tis next to a chattel slave to be a *legal* wife." Only when fellow abolitionist and women's rights activist Henry Blackwell began courting her in the 1850s did Stone's resolve weaken. When they married in 1855, though, Stone still made a feminist statement by keeping her maiden name. In 1857 Stone gave birth to a daughter, Alice Stone Blackwell, who would carry on the women's rights struggle when she became an adult. News of Stone's pregnancy, however, was met with exasperation by Susan B. Anthony, who believed that Stone's energy would be diverted from women's equality to motherhood. "Lucy," Anthony wrote, "*neither* of us have *time*—for such *per-*

sonal matters." Parenthood did force Stone to cut back on her lecturing, but she was unrepentant about her decision to have children. "I must make the path for my own feet," she wrote to Anthony. "I have no advice or explanation to make to *anybody.*"

As the years passed, Stone's marriage to Blackwell proved turbulent. The two lived apart on numerous occasions in subsequent decades. In addition, the family faced recurring financial difficulties stemming in part from Blackwell's unsuccessful investment schemes. Stone's strong principles also caused discomfort. Shortly after Alice's birth, Stone refused to pay a property tax bill in her name because, as she stated, "women suffer taxation yet have no representation." Unmoved by her rationale, the town seized her personal belongings and auctioned them.

Following the Civil War, Stone was thrust into the center of a heated debate in the suffragist movement over the Fifteenth Amendment. Radical suffragists such as Susan B. Anthony and Elizabeth Cady Stanton opposed the amendment because it failed to advance the cause of women in any way. Stone and others in the movement, however, supported the amendment as a vital tool in ensuring African American rights. As a leader of the American Woman Suffrage Association (AWSA), Stone labored mightily to defuse the conflict. But the organization split into two camps, with Stanton and Anthony withdrawing to form a rival group called the National Woman's Suffrage Association (NWSA). Stone's relations with Anthony, especially, were marked by much bitterness in the following decades.

Finding a Home

Though Stone had moved between several different residences and cities over the years, she chose to settle down in the early 1870s, buying a large home in Boston known as Pope's Hill. From there she oversaw publication of the *Woman's Journal* and directed the activities of the AWSA. Through careful management of her money, she was able to recover from her previous financial problems and even built up a sizable estate prior to her death.

Stone had suffered from severe headaches most of her life, and in later years her health problems multiplied. A bout with pneumonia nearly killed her in 1880, and problems with her heart and throat flared up over the following decade. Though relations between Stone and Anthony remained frosty, Stone reluctantly agreed to the merger of the AWSA and the rival

NWSA in 1890. Shortly thereafter Stone's condition worsened, and in 1893 she was diagnosed with stomach cancer. She died on October 18, 1893.

Sources

Gurko, Miriam. *The Ladies of Seneca Falls: The Birth of the Woman's Rights Movement.* New York: Macmillan, 1974.

Kerr, Andrea Moore. *Lucy Stone: Speaking Out for Equality.* New Brunswick, NJ: Rutgers University Press, 1992.

Million, Joelle. *Woman's Voice, Woman's Place: Lucy Stone and the Birth of the Woman's Rights Movement.* Westport, CT: Praeger, 2003.

Sherr, Lynn. *Susan B. Anthony: In Her Own Words.* New York: Times Books, 1995.

Sojourner Truth (c. 1797-1883)
Abolitionist and Women's Rights Activist

The woman who would later adopt the name Sojourner Truth was given the name Isabella when she was born around the year 1797 in Ulster County, New York. Isabella came into the world as a slave because her parents were slaves. Her father was known as James or Bomefree and her mother was known as Elizabeth or Mau Mau Bett. Both were the property of the Hardenbergh family, landowners who originally hailed from the Netherlands, so Isabella's first language was Dutch. At about age ten Isabella was separated from her parents and sold to another owner. Later, she became the property of the Dumont family in New Paltz, New York. She served them for about seventeen years, during which time she married a slave named Thomas and had five children.

Isabella obtained her freedom when she was about thirty years old. Though she was technically an escaped slave when she left the Dumonts, her freedom was ensured when New York enacted a ban on slavery. The emancipation of her children was delayed, however, because the new law forced younger slaves to work until their mid-twenties. Shortly after leaving the Dumonts, she learned that her son Peter had been sold to a slave owner in Alabama. With the help of antislavery activists, she went to court and won Peter's freedom. At about this same time Isabella underwent a religious conversion and devoted herself to an evangelical form of Christian Methodism. Religion was a central part of her life from then on, sometimes manifested in visions and messages from God.

In 1828 Isabella moved to New York City with Peter, where she worked as a household servant and began to preach at religious gatherings. She soon came under the influence of a man who called himself the Prophet Matthias and lived for more than a year in a cult-like commune near Mount Pleasant, New York. In the early 1840s a new revelation beckoned. "I went to the Lord and asked him to give me a new name," she later recalled in her autobiography. "And the Lord gave me Sojourner, because I was to travel up and down the land, showing the people their sins, and being a sign unto them."

Truth became an itinerant preacher for several months before joining a utopian community in Northampton, Massachusetts. There, Truth met abolitionists Frederick Douglass and William Lloyd Garrison, and she soon decided to become an antislavery speaker. Her first-hand experience of servitude, combined with her singing and public speaking skills, made her a popular spokesperson for the abolitionist cause.

In the late 1840s, Truth began dictating her life story to Olive Gilbert. When published in 1850, the *Narrative of Sojourner Truth* added to Truth's fame. It also gave her a measure of financial security. In fact, she used the profits from sales of her memoir to purchase her own home in Northampton, where she lived through the mid-1850s.

Truth and Women

Truth's abolitionist work put her in contact with a variety of women's rights activists, for the two movements worked closely together to advance their respective causes at mid-century. Truth thus emerged as a regular presence at early women's rights conventions, including an 1851 gathering in Akron, Ohio. Truth delivered a speech at this convention that remains one of the most famous statements on the strength and abilities of the female sex in American history. A version of Truth's address at this meeting was taken down by Frances Gage and later published in *History of Woman Suffrage* (see "Sojourner Truth's 'A'n't I a Woman' speech," p. 156.)

The speech illustrated Truth's power as an orator. Using simple, colloquial language she was able to cut to the heart of the matter in terms all could understand. Her physical stature added to her impact. She stood nearly six feet tall and showed little fear, even when standing before hostile audiences. These traits, along with her low, booming voice, led some critics to suggest that she was actually a man. When she was confronted by this charge at meeting in 1858, Truth bared her breasts and told the crowd she had suckled many a white babe during her years as a slave.

In the years following the Civil War, Truth was one of few activists who refused to separate the rights of African Americans from the rights of females. She rejected the argument that black voting rights were more crucial than women's suffrage as well as the notion that educated women were more deserving of the vote than unschooled blacks. Instead, Truth spoke for black women—a group that was often left out of the debates. "There is a great stir about colored men getting their rights, but not a word about colored women," she said in an 1867 speech. "If colored men get their rights, and not colored women theirs, you see colored men will be masters over the women, and it will be just as bad as it was before." She believed that African Americans and women should remain united, and she called for changes in the Fourteenth and Fifteenth Amendments that would address sexual as well as racial discrimination.

Aiding Former Slaves

Drawing upon her own experience, Truth knew that the newly freed slaves were going to require assistance in beginning their lives as free men and women. In fact, she began this work even before the Civil War ended, working with emancipated blacks in Virginia as part of the National Freedman's Relief Association. In 1870 she promoted a plan whereby the government would provide land in the western part of the country to former slaves. She spent several years making speeches and collecting signatures on behalf of her plan but failed to sway Congress. "Everybody says this is a good work, but nobody helps," she complained. Though government land was never obtained, Truth lent her assistance to the thousands of blacks who migrated to Kansas on their own in the late 1870s.

Truth had moved to Battle Creek, Michigan, in 1857, and she remained an off-and-on resident of the city over the following decades. Her first home in Battle Creek was part of yet another utopian community, Harmonia, which was formed by a spiritualist group that was an offshoot of the Quakers. In the final decade of her life Truth suffered partial paralysis and other health problems but she was cared for by three daughters who lived in Battle Creek. Though her travels were limited during this period, she welcomed many visitors who came to pay tribute to her. She died on November 26, 1883.

Sources

Fitch, Suzanne Pullon, and Roseann M. Mandziuk. *Sojourner Truth as Orator: Wit, Story, and Song.* Westport, CT: Greenwood, 1997.

Gilbert, Olive. *Narrative of Sojourner Truth.* 1850. Reprint, Mineola, NY: Dover, 1997.

Painter, Nell Irvin. *Sojourner Truth: A Life, A Symbol.* New York: W.W. Norton, 1996.

Stanton, Elizabeth Cady, Susan B. Anthony, and Matilda Joslyn Gage, eds. *History of Woman Suffrage.* Vol. 2, *1861-1876.* New York: Fowler & Wells, 1882.

Ida B. Wells-Barnett (1862-1931)
Journalist, Suffragist, and Civil Rights Activist

Ida B. Wells was born on July 16, 1862, in Holly Springs, Mississippi, the oldest of seven children born to James Wells and Elizabeth (Bell) Wells. Ida Wells was born into slavery, but the issuance of the Emancipation Proclamation later in 1862 and the final defeat of the Confederacy in 1865 brought freedom to the entire Wells family. After the war, Elizabeth and James Wells retained their old jobs as a cook and carpenter, respectively. Their children, meanwhile, were educated at Rust College, a school run by missionaries from the northern United States.

When Wells was sixteen, both of her parents and her youngest brother were killed in a yellow fever epidemic that swept through northern Mississippi. Forced to take care of her five younger brothers and sisters, she convinced a local school board that she was eighteen—the minimum age required for teachers—and began her career as an educator. Four years later, after her brothers had begun apprenticeships, she and her two sisters moved to Memphis, where Wells taught in the city's African-American schools until 1891.

Wells's activism began soon after she arrived in Memphis. After being removed from a first-class rail car because of her race, she filed suit against the train company. She initially won a $500 judgement only to have it reversed on appeal. In the mid-1880s she wrote a series of newspaper articles that bitterly protested the treatment of African Americans. Her fiery words, written under the pen name of Iola, captured national attention, as did her dismissal from the Memphis school system after she openly criticized its segregation-based inequities.

On no subject was Wells more outspoken than the murders carried out by white mobs against African Americans on a regular basis throughout the South. In *Free Speech*, a black paper she helped launch, Wells publicized and denounced the lynchings taking place in Memphis and throughout the South.

After a friend was killed by vigilantes, she urged blacks to leave Memphis, "a town which will neither protect our lives and property, nor give us a fair trial in the courts, but take us out and murder us in cold blood when accused by a white person." In another editorial, she stated that blacks were justified in using violence to avenge lynchings.

Exiled from the South

Wells's strong opinions made her a controversial figure. She began carrying a pistol for protection, but she did not moderate her views. In 1892 she penned an editorial that rejected the stereotypical idea that black men were a threat to white women and instead suggested that some white women were attracted to black men. In response, a mob destroyed the *Free Speech* offices, and death threats were made against Wells. She received this news in New York City, where she was visiting, and decided it was too dangerous to return to the South. She lived in the northern United States for the rest of her life. Initially she based herself in New York and conducted speaking tours in Europe to publicize the violence being carried out against African Americans. A few years later she relocated to Chicago. This move coincided with her 1895 marriage to lawyer Ferdinand L. Barnett, with whom she eventually had four children.

Wells-Barnett continued her anti-lynching efforts into the twentieth century and was also involved in a variety of other causes. She attempted, with partial success, to include black women in the World's Columbian Exposition in 1893, organized a Chicago women's club, and fought against a plan to segregate the Chicago schools. In 1909 she played a key role in the establishment of the National Association for the Advancement of Colored People (NAACP) and served on its executive committee. She later left the group because she felt that it was not being forceful enough in protecting the rights of African Americans. This stance was typical of Wells-Barnett, who was known for her uncompromising, militant positions in the pursuit of racial and sexual equality.

Promoting Women's Suffrage

Wells-Barnett recognized the power of the ballot as an engine of social change, so she labored mightily to give the vote to women. She became friendly with Susan B. Anthony in the 1890s, and Anthony once described Wells-Barnett as a woman with "a special call for special work." Nonetheless,

Anthony consciously chose to exclude blacks from the National American Woman Suffrage Association in the 1890s in an effort to curry favor with white citizens. Wells-Barnett harshly condemned Anthony's decision.

Battling against racial discrimination within the women's rights community became an ongoing experience for Wells-Barnett and other black suffragists. One of the most famous incidents of this kind took place in March 1913, when the Washington, D.C., suffrage parade took place. As a member of the Women's Suffrage Association of Illinois, Wells-Barnett intended to march with other Illinois suffragists. In an effort to appease Southern activists, though, parade organizers wanted black participants to march separately, at the end of the parade. Wells-Barnett refused to accept this segregationist arrangement. "If the Illinois women do not take a stand now in this great democratic parade," she said, "then the colored women are lost." As the procession began, she slipped out of the crowd and joined the white marchers from her home state. Wells-Barnett remained with them for the full parade.

In the 1910s women in Illinois gained certain limited voting rights that allowed them to vote for university trustees and, later, in municipal elections. Determined to seize these opportunities, Wells-Barnett urged fellow African Americans to participate in the political process to the greatest degree possible. An important step in this direction was the formation of the Alpha Suffrage Club in 1913. The club helped get out the black vote and became a significant political force in the city. In 1914, for example, the Alphas played a crucial role in an African American candidate's successful bid for a seat as a Chicago alderman. This triumph set an important precedent, for it showed—even before the granting of nationwide suffrage—that black female voters were a potentially powerful political voice that could influence elections.

Wells-Barnett remained active in civic and political affairs after passage of the Nineteenth Amendment. In 1924 she made a bid for president of the National Association of Colored Women but was defeated. Six years later she ran for a seat in the Illinois senate as an independent but finished well behind the major-party candidates. The following year she suffered kidney problems and died on March 25, 1931, after a brief hospitalization.

Sources
Alexander, Adele Logan. "Adella Hunt Logan, the Tuskegee Woman's Club, and African Americans in the Suffrage Movement." In *Votes for Women!: The Woman Suffrage Movement in Tennessee, the South, and the Nation.* Edited by Marjorie Spruill Wheeler. Knoxville, TN: University of Tennessee Press, 1995.

McMurry, Linda O. *To Keep the Waters Troubled: The Life of Ida B. Wells.* New York: Oxford University Press, 1998.

Terborg-Penn, Rosalyn. *African American Women in the Struggle for the Vote, 1850-1920.* Bloomington, IN: Indiana University Press, 1998.

Wells-Barnett, Ida B. *Crusade for Justice: The Autobiography of Ida B. Wells.* Chicago: University of Chicago Press, 1970.

Woodrow Wilson (1856-1924)
President of the United States during Ratification of the Nineteenth Amendment

Thomas Woodrow Wilson was born in Staunton, Virginia, on December 28, 1856, the son of Joseph Ruggles Wilson and Jessie (Woodrow) Wilson. Wilson spent most of his childhood in Augusta, Georgia, where his father served as minister of a Presbyterian church. The elder Wilson supported Southern secession, and after the Civil War began in 1861 he served briefly as a chaplain in the Confederate Army. The war did not alter the family's fortunes to any great extent, and at age eighteen, Woodrow was able to begin his college studies. He would remain part of the academic world for the next thirty-six years, pausing only for a brief, unsuccessful attempt at becoming a trial lawyer. He received his undergraduate degree from the College of New Jersey (which later became Princeton University) and earned a Ph.D. from Johns Hopkins University in Baltimore in 1886, specializing in constitutional law. After joining the faculty at Princeton in 1890, he developed into a distinguished educator and published several well-regarded books, including *History of the American People*. In 1885 he married Ellen Louise Axson, with whom he eventually had three daughters.

In 1902 Wilson became president of Princeton. He immediately set out to overhaul the university's education system by altering the curriculum, changing teaching methods, and reshaping student social life. Many of these efforts were successful, but Wilson also encountered opposition and saw some of his plans blocked by the school's board of trustees.

In 1910 powerbrokers in the New Jersey Democratic Party convinced Wilson to run for governor, believing that he could be easily controlled. Wilson proved more reform-oriented than they expected, however. He fended off the political bosses, allied himself with the party's progressive wing, and swept to victory. Once in office he pushed through legislation on worker's compensation, regulation of utilities, and reforms to the state's education system. These accomplishments made him a rising star in Democratic politics, and at the 1912 convention, he emerged as his party's presidential nominee. In the November election, Wilson defeated both William Howard Taft and Theodore Roosevelt to become president of the United States.

Wilson and the Woman Voter

Though he was in some respects a political reformer, Wilson was not a proponent of women's suffrage at the time he took office. When asked his stance on suffrage during the 1912 presidential campaign, he said "ladies, this is a very arguable question, and my mind is in the middle of the argument." This noncommittal approach was shared by many male politicians of this era.

Wilson probably would have preferred to stay "in the middle of the argument" forever, but suffragists began pushing him on the issue almost as soon as he was in office. In March 1913 Alice Paul and several other members of the National American Woman Suffrage Association (NAWSA) met with Wilson at the White House. The group asked the president to include women's suffrage on his agenda for congressional action. Wilson claimed that he was insufficiently familiar with the arguments being put forth by the pro- and anti-suffrage camps, and he asked for more time to study the issue.

When suffragists continued to press him on the issue, Wilson endorsed the official position of the Democratic Party, which held that suffrage was a "states' rights" issue that should be decided by each state on its own. But while Wilson expressed opposition to a constitutional amendment on suffrage that would apply to the whole nation, he eventually acknowledged a personal belief that women should have the right to vote. In 1915, in fact, he cast a vote in favor of a suffrage measure in his home state of New Jersey.

During his reelection bid in 1916, Wilson addressed the NAWSA convention in Atlantic City—a clear indication that he took the suffrage movement seriously. "We feel the tide [of suffrage]," he declared. "We rejoice in the strength of it; and we shall not quarrel in the long run as to the method of it." This cautious encouragement was more than any previous U.S. president had offered.

It was not, however, an explicit endorsement of the suffrage amendment. Until he took that step, the National Woman's Party (NWP) remained intent on confronting the president about his lack of support and opposing the Democrats in elections. In December 1916 the NWP disrupted Wilson's address at the Capitol. The following month, Alice Paul and the NWP leadership initiated widely publicized picketing activities outside the White House. The president made few public comments about the picketers, but it is reasonable to believe that he was not pleased with their actions. Historians speculate about whether or not the president or his immediate staff played a direct role in the arrest and imprisonment of the demonstrators. Some believe that they did, but others contend that local officials acted on their own. In any event, Woodrow Wilson eventually did become a supporter of the Nineteenth Amendment, and his support was essential in its passage.

War and Disappointment

Of course, women's suffrage was only one of many issues that Wilson grappled with during his tenure in the White House. His presidency was defined by World War I. When the conflict began in 1914, Wilson advocated a policy of neutrality, and he tried to negotiate a settlement between the warring factions. A key part of his successful reelection bid in 1916 was the motto "he kept us out of war."

Yet by early 1917 Wilson's perspective on events in Europe had changed. He led the nation into the conflict later that year, and the arrival of American troops in Europe proved decisive. By the time the war ended in November 1918, the United States had proven itself a global power, and Woodrow Wilson was poised to reshape the postwar world. His Fourteen Point program, which called for the establishment of democratic governments and promoted the right of self-determination, was a central part of the Paris Peace Conference that followed the war. Wilson also helped establish the League of Nations, which was designed to prevent further wars. In recognition of these efforts, Wilson later received the Nobel Peace Prize.

In the end, however, both the peace negotiations and the League of Nations were disappointments. The final Treaty of Versailles placed heavy financial burdens on Germany, which destabilized the country and later helped bring Adolf Hitler to power. In the United States, the Senate refused to approve the treaty and blocked the United States from joining the League of Nations. America's absence weakened the league, and it proved ineffectual in preventing a return to militarism in the 1920s and 1930s.

While frantically promoting the treaty and the League of Nations, Wilson suffered a stroke in 1919 that left him partially paralyzed. His second wife, Edith Bolling Galt, who he had married in 1915 following the death of his first wife, played a large role in the final year of his presidency. He did not seek reelection in 1920, and his postwar initiatives were swept aside by his successor, Republican Warren G. Harding. He never regained his health, and his final years were spent in seclusion in Washington, D.C. He died there on February 3, 1924.

Sources

Ford, Linda G. *Iron-Jawed Angels: The Suffrage Militancy of the National Woman's Party, 1912-1920.* Lanham, MD: University Press of America, 1991.

Heckscher, August. *Woodrow Wilson.* New York: Charles Scribner's Sons, 1991.

Irwin, Inez Hayes. *The Story of Alice Paul and the National Woman's Party.* Fairfax, VA: Denlinger's Publishers, 1977.

Lunardini, Christine A. *From Equal Suffrage to Equal Rights: Alice Paul and the National Woman's Party, 1910-1928.* New York: New York University Press, 1986.

Victoria C. Woodhull (1838-1927)
Women's Rights Advocate and Presidential Candidate

Born Victoria Claflin on September 23, 1838, in Homer, Ohio, Woodhull was the sixth of nine surviving children born to Reuben Buckman "Buck" Claflin and Roxanna (Hummel) Claflin. Led by their father, the Claflin family earned a threadbare existence through dubious schemes such as fortune telling, blackmail, and theft. Woodhull's mother was known to lapse into fits of religious ecstasy, and Victoria later claimed, according to her own account, that she inherited her mother's ability to perceive the supernatural.

Buck Claflin eventually put both Victoria and her younger sister Tennessee to work as child spiritualists, supplementing their earnings by selling bottles of "Life Elixir." Woodhull later described herself as a "child without a childhood," forced to support her family and endure beatings from her father as the Claflins traveled from town to town in the Midwest. Some of her writings also suggest that her father sexually abused her. Her solace, she claimed, came from her spirit guides, one of whom promised her that she would one day "rise to a great distinction,… that she would win great wealth,… that she would become the ruler of her people."

At age fifteen Victoria married Canning Woodhull, a doctor twelve years her senior who turned out to be an alcoholic and morphine addict. The marriage produced a lot of misery and two children—one of whom was mentally retarded. Again Victoria was forced to be the breadwinner, working as a spiritual clairvoyant in the Midwest and as an actress and seamstress during the family's tenure in San Francisco. At times, her family's struggles forced Woodhull into situations that verged on prostitution, according to historian Barbara Goldsmith in *Other Powers*. By the early 1860s Woodhull could tolerate her husband's addictions no longer, and the marriage came to an end.

Over the next eight years Woodhull employed her spiritualist skills in many different midwestern cities. In St. Louis Woodhull met her second husband, James Harvey Blood. He proved more supportive than the previous men in her life, but the couple's so-called free love relationship was far from conventional. Tennessee Claflin began traveling with Woodhull and Blood in the mid-1800s, having finally fled her parents' mistreatment. From that point on, the sisters were inseparable. In 1868 Woodhull claimed that her spirit guide instructed her to relocate to New York City.

Befriending the Commodore

Of all the strange twists in Woodhull's life, the strangest took place over the next few years. After arriving in New York, Woodhull and her sister resumed their trade as clairvoyants. This brought them in contact with millionaire Cornelius Vanderbilt, an avowed spiritualist, who was then in his mid-seventies. Known as "the Commodore" because he had made much of his fortune in shipping, Vanderbilt took a liking to the two attractive young women and struck up a romantic relationship with Tennessee (now going by the name "Tennie C."). Woodhull, on the other hand, earned Vanderbilt's esteem by allegedly connecting him to the spirit of his deceased mother and also by providing him with some remarkably profitable predictions on stock investments.

As time passed, Vanderbilt gave the sisters a portion of the profits on his stock trades and he eventually assisted them in setting up their own investment firm. When it opened in 1870 Woodhull and Claflin's combined assets were worth more than $700,000. As the first women on Wall Street, they received extensive coverage from newspapers across the country. Susan B. Anthony paid them a visit on behalf of her paper *The Revolution.* When Anthony asked if they intended to join the suffrage movement, Woodhull assured the long-time suffragist that she intended to add her voice to the cause.

Over the ensuing months Woodhull made good on her promise. In a controversial address to members of Congress—during which she contended that women already had the legal right to vote—and throughout a quixotic presidential candidacy, Woodhull portrayed herself as a woman of action. At times she consciously contrasted herself to the veteran suffragists who by that point had fallen to bickering with one another. "While others argued the equality of women with man, I proved it by successfully engaging in business," she wrote in *Woodhull and Claflin's Weekly,* a newspaper co-founded by her and her sister Tennessee. "I therefore claim the right to speak for the unenfranchised women of the country."

Woodhull claimed that many of her pronouncements and writings came to her while she was in a trance state, but historians believe that many of her speeches and newspaper articles were written by others—Senator Benjamin Butler, free-love advocate Stephen Pearl Andrews, and Woodhull's husband, James Harvey Blood. But to dismiss her as a phony, as many of her opponents did at the time, was to underestimate her dedication, intelligence, and charisma. She was able to enchant large audiences and move jaded politicians to consider her views. Though many dismissed her activities as publicity stunts, she seemed to truly believe in her cause.

In the early 1870s, however, Woodhull's family entanglements came back to haunt her. She allowed her entire family, including her parents and first husband, to establish residence in her New York mansion. This proved disastrous on many levels. Her mother filed a lawsuit against James Harvey Blood, which led to a public airing of Woodhull's turbulent marriages. In addition, her father stole money from the investment firm and her alcoholic sister jeered Woodhull at public lectures. Previously, Victoria and Tennie C. had created false histories for themselves that claimed they were from a wealthy New York family and that Tennie C. had studied law. When the press began digging into the family's background, they found a much different story.

Finally, as her money ran out and her presidential campaign was ignored or belittled, Woodhull lashed out at her enemies. In November 1872 she published a story in *Woodhull and Claflin's Weekly* charging that Henry Ward Beecher, an influential minister and suffragist, had carried on an adulterous affair with Elizabeth Tilton, the wife of another prominent suffragist. Woodhull's revelation badly damaged the suffrage movement in the court of public opinion, and it led authorities to arrest both her and her sister for sending obscenity through the mail.

Joins the English Aristocracy

After finally being acquitted of obscenity charges in 1874—after seven months in jail—Woodhull was exhausted and penniless. She spent several years attempting to earn a living on the speaking circuit, but she abandoned her themes of free love and women's rights in favor of a odd blend of religious and scientific topics that proved far less popular. She and Blood divorced in 1876. Two years later, she met John Biddulph Martin, a member of a wealthy British family, during a speaking tour in England. They were married in 1883 and settled in London. Tennie C. Claflin, meanwhile, married into English royalty, becoming Lady Cook, the Viscountess of Montserrat.

Woodhull attempted two more presidential campaigns, in 1880 and 1892, but they were weak efforts concocted in part to give her more social prestige in Britain, where she had generally been scorned by her husband's upper-class peers. She also resorted to more fabrications, including changing her last name to Woodhall and creating a false family tree. These efforts to gain acceptance in England came to naught, but she did inherit her husband's country estate upon his death in 1897. She oversaw it until her own death on June 9, 1927.

Sources

Gabriel, Mary. *Notorious Victoria: The Life of Victoria Woodhull, Uncensored.* Chapel Hill, NC: Algonquin Books, 1998.

Goldsmith, Barbara. *Other Powers: The Age of Suffrage, Spiritualism, and the Scandalous Victoria Woodhull.* New York: Knopf, 1998.

PRIMARY SOURCES

Declaration of Sentiments and Resolutions, 1848 Seneca Falls Convention

The pioneers of the women's suffrage movement issued the following declaration and resolutions as part of the historic Woman's Rights Convention held in Seneca Falls, New York, on July 19 and 20, 1848. This gathering is generally considered the beginning of the women's suffrage movement in the United States. The participants based this document on the Declaration of Independence—which announced the United States' intention to leave the British Empire and form an independent nation—because they felt it was time for women to make a similar break from traditional roles.

Declaration of Sentiments

When, in the course of human events, it becomes necessary for one portion of the family of man to assume among the people of the earth a position different from that which they have hitherto occupied, but one to which the laws of nature and of nature's God entitle them, a decent respect to the opinions of mankind requires that they should declare the causes that impel them to such a course.

We hold these truths to be self-evident: that all men and women are created equal; that they are endowed by their Creator with certain inalienable rights; that among these are life, liberty, and the pursuit of happiness; that to secure these rights governments are instituted, deriving their just powers from the consent of the governed. Whenever any form of government becomes destructive of these ends, it is the right of those who suffer from it to refuse allegiance to it, and to insist upon the institution of a new government, laying its foundation on such principles, and organizing its powers in such form, as to them shall seem most likely to effect their safety and happiness. Prudence, indeed, will dictate that governments long established should not be changed for light and transient causes; and accordingly all experience hath shown that mankind are more disposed to suffer, while evils are sufferable, than to right themselves by abolishing the forms to which they were accustomed. But when a long train of abuses and usurpations, pursuing invariably the same object evinces a design to reduce them under absolute despotism, it is their duty to throw off such government, and to provide new guards for their future security. Such has been the patient sufferance of the women under this government, and such is now the necessity which constrains them to demand the equal station to which they are entitled.

The history of mankind is a history of repeated injuries and usurpations on the part of man toward woman, having in direct object the establishment of an absolute tyranny over her. To prove this, let facts be submitted to a candid world.

He has never permitted her to exercise her inalienable right to the elective franchise.

He has compelled her to submit to laws, in the formation of which she had no voice.

He has withheld from her rights which are given to the most ignorant and degraded men—both natives and foreigners.

Having deprived her of this first right of a citizen, the elective franchise, thereby leaving her without representation in the halls of legislation, he has oppressed her on all sides.

He has made her, if married, in the eye of the law, civilly dead.

He has taken from her all right in property, even to the wages she earns.

He has made her, morally, an irresponsible being, as she can commit many crimes with impunity, provided they be done in the presence of her husband. In the covenant of marriage, she is compelled to promise obedience to her husband, he becoming, to all intents and purposes, her master—the law giving him power to deprive her of her liberty, and to administer chastisement.

He has so framed the laws of divorce, as to what shall be the proper causes, and in case of separation, to whom the guardianship of the children shall be given, as to be wholly regardless of the happiness of women—the law, in all cases, going upon a false supposition of the supremacy of man, and giving all power into his hands.

After depriving her of all rights as a married woman, if single, and the owner of property, he has taxed her to support a government which recognizes her only when her property can be made profitable to it.

He has monopolized nearly all the profitable employments, and from those she is permitted to follow, she receives but a scanty remuneration. He closes against her all the avenues to wealth and distinction which he considers most honorable to himself. As a teacher of theology, medicine, or law, she is not known.

He has denied her the facilities for obtaining a thorough education, all colleges being closed against her.

He allows her in Church, as well as State, but a subordinate position, claiming Apostolic authority for her exclusion from the ministry, and, with some exceptions, from any public participation in the affairs of the Church.

He has created a false public sentiment by giving to the world a different code of morals for men and women, by which moral delinquencies which exclude women from society, are not only tolerated, but deemed of little account in man.

He has usurped the prerogative of Jehovah himself, claiming it as his right to assign for her a sphere of action, when that belongs to her conscience and to her God.

He has endeavored, in every way that he could, to destroy her confidence in her own powers, to lessen her self-respect, and to make her willing to lead a dependent and abject life.

Now, in view of this entire disfranchisement of one-half the people of this country, their social and religious degradation—in view of the unjust laws above mentioned, and because women do feel themselves aggrieved, oppressed, and fraudulently deprived of their most sacred rights, we insist that they have immediate admission to all the rights and privileges which belong to them as citizens of the United States.

In entering upon the great work before us, we anticipate no small amount of misconception, misrepresentation, and ridicule; but we shall use every instrumentality within our power to effect our object. We shall employ agents, circulate tracts, petition the State and National legislatures, and endeavor to enlist the pulpit and the press in our behalf. We hope this Convention will be followed by a series of Conventions embracing every part of the country.

The following resolutions were discussed by Lucretia Mott, Thomas and Mary Ann McClintock, Amy Post, Catharine A. F. Stebbins, and others, and were adopted:

WHEREAS, The great precept of nature is conceded to be, that "man shall pursue his own true and substantial happiness." [Legal scholar Sir William] Blackstone in his Commentaries remarks, that this law of Nature being coeval with mankind, and dictated by God himself, is of course superior in obligation to any other. It is binding over all the globe, in all countries and at all times; no human laws are of any validity if contrary to this, and such of them as are valid, derive all their force, and all their validity, and all their authority, mediately and immediately, from this original; therefore,

Resolved, That such laws as conflict, in any way, with the true and substantial happiness of woman, are contrary to the great precept of nature and of no validity, for this is "superior in obligation to any other."

Resolved, That all laws which prevent woman from occupying such a station in society as her conscience shall dictate, or which place her in a position inferior to that of man, are contrary to the great precept of nature, and therefore of no force or authority.

Resolved, That woman is man's equal—was intended to be so by the Creator, and the highest good of the race demands that she should be recognized as such.

Resolved, That the women of this country ought to be enlightened in regard to the laws under which they live, that they may no longer publish their degradation by declaring themselves satisfied with their present position, nor their ignorance, by asserting that they have all the rights they want.

Resolved, That inasmuch as man, while claiming for himself intellectual superiority, does accord to woman moral superiority, it is pre-eminently his duty to encourage her to speak and teach, as she has an opportunity, in all religious assemblies.

Resolved, That the same amount of virtue, delicacy, and refinement of behavior that is required of woman in the social state, should also be required of man, and the same transgressions should be visited with equal severity on both man and woman.

Resolved, That the objection of indelicacy and impropriety, which is so often brought against woman when she addresses a public audience, comes with a very ill-grace from those who encourage, by their attendance, her appearance on the stage, in the concert, or in feats of the circus.

Resolved, That woman has too long rested satisfied in the circumscribed limits which corrupt customs and a perverted application of the Scriptures have marked out for her, and that it is time she should move in the enlarged sphere which her great Creator has assigned her.

Resolved, That it is the duty of the women of this country to secure to themselves their sacred right to the elective franchise.

Resolved, That the equality of human rights results necessarily from the fact of the identity of the race in capabilities and responsibilities.

Resolved, therefore, That, being invested by the Creator with the same capabilities, and the same consciousness of responsibility for their exercise, it is demonstrably the right and duty of woman, equally with man, to promote every righteous cause by every righteous means; and especially in regard to the great subjects of morals and religion; it is self-evidently her right to participate with her brother in teaching them, both in private and in public, by writing and by speaking, by any instrumentalities proper to be used, and in any assemblies proper to be held; and this being a self-evident truth growing out of the divinely implanted principles of human nature, any custom or authority adverse to it, whether modern or wearing the hoary sanction of antiquity, is to be regarded as a self-evident falsehood, and at war with mankind.

At the last session Lucretia Mott offered and spoke to the following resolution:

Resolved, That the speedy success of our cause depends upon the zealous and untiring efforts of both men and women, for the overthrow of the monopoly of the pulpit, and for the securing to woman an equal participation with men in the various trades, professions, and commerce.

The only resolution that was not unanimously adopted was the ninth, urging the women of the country to secure to themselves the elective franchise. Those who took part in the debate feared a demand for the right to vote would defeat others they deemed more rational, and make the whole movement ridiculous.

But Mrs. Stanton and Frederick Douglass seeing that the power to choose rulers and make laws, was the right by which all others could be secured, persistently advocated the resolution, and at last carried it by a small majority.

Source: Stanton, Elizabeth Cady, Susan B. Anthony, and Matilda Joslyn Gage, eds. *History of Woman Suffrage.* Vol. 1, *1848-1861.* New York: Fowler & Wells, 1881.

Sojourner Truth's "A'n't I a Woman" Speech

The following account by suffragist Frances D. Gage is the most commonly published retelling of Sojourner Truth's famous "A'n't I a Woman" speech. A former slave, Truth made the speech before the women's rights convention in Akron, Ohio, in May 1851. In it, she presents a powerful case for women's rights and responds to the arguments put forth by anti-suffrage speakers. Some historians believe that Gage's version exaggerates Truth's African American dialect, however, and is therefore a somewhat inaccurate translation of the way she actually spoke.

The leaders of the movement trembled on seeing a tall, gaunt black woman in a gray dress and white turban, surmounted with an uncouth sun-bonnet, march deliberately into the church, walk with the air of a queen up the aisle, and take her seat upon the pulpit steps. A buzz of disapprobation was heard all over the house, and there fell on the listening ear, "An abolition affair!" "Woman's rights and niggers!" "I told you so!" "Go it, darkey!"

I chanced on that occasion to wear my first laurels in public life as president of the meeting. At my request order was restored, and the business of the Convention went on. Morning, afternoon, and evening exercises came and went. Through all these sessions old Sojourner, quiet and reticent as the "Lybian Statue," sat crouched against the wall on the corner of the pulpit stairs, her sun-bonnet shading her eyes, her elbows on her knees, her chin resting upon her broad, hard palms. At intermission she was busy selling the "Life of Sojourner Truth," a narrative of her own strange and adventurous life. Again and again, timorous and trembling ones came to me and said, with earnestness, "Don't let her speak, Mrs. Gage, it will ruin us. Every newspaper in the land will have our cause mixed up with abolition and niggers, and we shall be utterly denounced." My only answer was, "We shall see when the time comes."

The second day the work waxed warm. Methodist, Baptist, Episcopal, Presbyterian, and Universalist ministers came in to hear and discuss the resolutions presented. One claimed superior rights and privileges for man, on the ground of "superior intellect,'" another, because of the "manhood of Christ; if God had desired the equality of woman, He would have given some token of His will through the birth, life, and death of the Savior." Another gave us a theological view of the "sin of our first mother."

There were very few women in those days who dared to "speak in meeting"; and the august teachers of the people were seemingly getting the better of us, while the boys in the galleries, and the sneerers among the pews, were hugely enjoying the discomfiture, as they supposed, of the "strong-minded." Some of the tender-skinned friends were on the point of losing dignity, and the atmosphere betokened a storm. When, slowly from her seat in the corner rose Sojourner Truth, who, till now, had scarcely lifted her head. "Don't let her speak!" gasped half a dozen in my ear. She moved slowly and solemnly to the front, laid her old bonnet at her feet, and turned her great speaking eyes to me. There was a hissing sound of disapprobation above and below. I rose and announced "Sojourner Truth," and begged the audience to keep silence for a few moments.

The tumult subsided at once, and every eye was fixed on this almost Amazon form, which stood nearly six feet high, head erect, and eyes piercing the upper air like one in a dream. At her first word there was a profound hush. She spoke in deep tones, which, though not loud, reached every ear in the house, and away through the throng at the doors and windows.

"Wall, chilern, whar dar is so much racket dar must be somethin' out o' kilter. I tink dat 'twixt de niggers of de Souf and de womin at de Norf, all talkin' 'bout rights, de white men will be in a fix pretty soon. But what's all dis here talkin' 'bout?

"Dat man ober dar say dat womin needs to be helped into carriages, and lifted ober ditches, and to hab de best place everywhar. Nobody eber helps me into carriages, or ober mud-puddles, or gibs me any best place!" And raising herself to her full height, and her voice to a pitch like rolling thunder, she asked, "And a'n't I a woman? Look at me! Look at my arm! (and she bared her right arm to the shoulder, showing her tremendous muscular power). I have ploughed, and planted, and gathered into barns, and no man could head me! And a'n't I a woman? I could work as much and eat as much as a man—when I could get it—and bear de lash as well! And a'n't I a woman? I have borne thirteen chilern, and seen 'em mos' all sold off to slavery, and when I cried out with my mother's grief, none but Jesus heard me! And a'n't I a woman?

"Den dey talks 'bout dis ting in de head; what dis dey call it?" ("Intellect," whispered some one near.) "Dat's it, honey. What's dat got to do wid womin's rights or nigger's rights? If my cup won't hold but a pint, and yourn holds a quart, wouldn't ye be mean not to let me have my little half-measure full?" And she pointed her significant finger, and sent a keen glance at the minister who had made the argument. The cheering was long and loud.

"Den dat little man in black dar, he say women can't have as much rights as men, 'cause Christ wan't a woman! Whar did your Christ come from?"

157

Rolling thunder couldn't have stilled that crowd, as did those deep, wonderful tones, as she stood there with outstretched arms and eyes of fire. Raising her voice still louder, she repeated, "Whar did your Christ come from? From God and a woman! Man had nothin' to do wid Him." Oh, what a rebuke that was to that little man.

Turning again to another objector, she took up the defense of Mother Eve. I can not follow her through it all. It was pointed, and witty, and solemn; eliciting at almost every sentence deafening applause; and she ended by asserting: "If de fust woman God ever made was strong enough to turn de world upside down all alone, dese women togedder (and she glanced her eye over the platform) ought to be able to turn it back, and get it right side up again! And now dey is asking to do it, de men better let 'em." Long-continued cheering greeted this. "Bleeged to ye for hearin' on me, and now ole Sojourner han't got nothin' more to say."

Amid roars of applause, she returned to her corner, leaving more than one of us with streaming eyes, and hearts beating with gratitude. She had taken us up in her strong arms and carried us safely over the slough of difficulty turning the whole tide in our favor. I have never in my life seen anything like the magical influence that subdued the mobbish spirit of the day, and turned the sneers and jeers of an excited crowd into notes of respect and admiration. Hundreds rushed up to shake hands with her, and congratulate the glorious old mother, and bid her God-speed on her mission of "testifyin' agin concerning the wickedness of this 'ere people."

Source: Stanton, Elizabeth Cady, Susan B. Anthony, and Matilda Joslyn Gage, eds. *History of Woman Suffrage.* Vol. 1, *1848-1861*. New York: Fowler & Wells, 1881.

Elizabeth Cady Stanton Addresses the 1869 National Woman Suffrage Convention

After the Civil War ended, reformers became locked in a heated debate about expanding the right to vote. Women's suffrage pioneers felt that it was an ideal time to enfranchise women. But abolition leaders argued that women should wait until voting rights had been secured for African American men. In the following excerpt from a speech made on January 19, 1869, Elizabeth Cady Stanton urges a new constitutional amendment to enfranchise women. She also maintains that educated women are more deserving of the vote than certain groups of uneducated men, particularly the "lower orders of foreigners" and former slaves.

I urge a speedy adoption of a Sixteenth Amendment for the following reasons:

1. A government, based on the principle of caste and class, can not stand. The aristocratic idea, in any form, is opposed to the genius of our free institutions, to our own declaration of rights, and to the civilization of the age. All artificial distinctions, whether of family, blood, wealth, color, or sex, are equally oppressive to the subject classes, and equally destructive to national life and prosperity. Governments based on every form of aristocracy, on every degree and variety of inequality, have been tried in despotisms, monarchies, and republics, and all alike have perished. In the panorama of the past behold the mighty nations that have risen, one by one, but to fall. Behold their temples, thrones, and pyramids, their gorgeous palaces and stately monuments now crumbled all to dust. Behold every monarch in Europe at this very hour trembling on his throne. Behold the republics on this Western continent convulsed, distracted, divided, the hosts scattered, the leaders fallen, the scouts lost in the wilderness, the once inspired prophets blind and dumb, while on all sides the cry is echoed, "Republicanism is a failure," though that great principle of a government "by the people, of the people, for the people," has never been tried. Thus far, all nations have been built on caste and failed. Why, in this hour of reconstruction, with the experience of generations before us, make another experiment in the same direction? If serfdom, peasantry, and slavery have shattered kingdoms, deluged continents with blood, scattered republics like dust before the wind, and rent our own Union asunder, what kind of a government, think you, American statesmen, you can build, with the mothers of the race crouching at your feet, while iron-heeled peasants, serfs, and slaves, exalted by your hands, tread our

inalienable rights into the dust? While all men, everywhere, are rejoicing in new-found liberties, shall woman alone be denied the rights, privileges, and immunities of citizenship?… Of all kinds of aristocracy, that of sex is the most odious and unnatural; invading, as it does, our homes, desecrating our family altars, dividing those whom God has joined together, exalting the son above the mother who bore him, and subjugating, everywhere, moral power to brute force. Such a government would not be worth the blood and treasure so freely poured out in its long struggles for freedom.…

2. I urge a Sixteenth Amendment, because "manhood suffrage" or a man's government, is civil, religious, and social disorganization. The male element is a destructive force, stern, selfish, aggrandizing, loving war, violence, conquest, acquisition, breeding in the material and moral world alike discord, disorder, disease, and death. See what a record of blood and cruelty the pages of history reveal! Through what slavery, slaughter, and sacrifice, through what inquisitions and imprisonments, pains and persecutions, black codes and gloomy creeds, the soul of humanity has struggled for the centuries, while mercy has veiled her face and all hearts have been dead alike to love and hope! The male element has held high carnival thus far, it has fairly run riot from the beginning, overpowering the feminine element everywhere, crushing out all the diviner qualities in human nature, until we know but little of true manhood and womanhood, of the latter comparatively nothing, for it has scarce been recognized as a power until within the last century. Society is but the reflection of man himself, untempered by woman's thought, the hard iron rule we feel alike in the church, the state, and the home. No one need wonder at the disorganization, at the fragmentary condition of everything, when we remember that man, who represents but half a complete being, with but half an idea on every subject, has undertaken the absolute control of all sublunary matters.

People object to the demands of those whom they choose to call the strong-minded, because they say, "the right of suffrage will make the women masculine." That is just the difficulty in which we are involved to-day. Though disfranchised we have few women in the best sense, we have simply so many reflections, varieties, and dilutions of the masculine gender. The strong, natural characteristics of womanhood are repressed and ignored in dependence, for so long as man feeds woman she will try to please the giver and adapt herself to his condition. To keep a foothold in society woman must be as near like man as possible, reflect his ideas, opinions, virtues, motives, prejudices, and vices.…

We ask woman's enfranchisement, as the first step toward the recognition of that essential element in government that can only secure the health, strength, and prosperity of the nation. Whatever is done to lift woman to her true position will help to usher in a new day of peace and perfection for the race.... If the civilization of the age calls for an extension of the suffrage, surely a government of the most virtuous, educated men and women would better represent the whole, and protect the interests of all than could the representation of either sex alone. But government gains no new element of strength in admitting all men to the ballot-box, for we have too much of the man-power there already. We see this in every department of legislation, and it is a common remark, that unless some new virtue is infused into our public life the nation is doomed to destruction. Will the foreign element, the dregs of China, Germany, England, Ireland, and Africa supply this needed force, or the nobler types of American womanhood who have taught our presidents, senators, and congressmen the rudiments of all they know?

3. I urge a Sixteenth Amendment because, when "manhood suffrage" is established from Maine to California, woman has reached the lowest depths of political degradation. So long as there is a disfranchised class in this country, and that class its women, a man's government is worse than a white man's government with suffrage limited by property and educational qualification, because in proportion as you multiply the rulers, the conditions of the politically ostracised is more hopeless and degraded. John Stuart Mill, in his work on "Liberty," shows that the condition of one disfranchised man in a nation is worse than when the whole nation is under one man, because in the latter case, if the one man is despotic, the nation can easily throw him off, but what can one man do with a nation of tyrants over him? If American women find it hard to bear the oppressions of their own Saxon fathers, the best orders of manhood, what may they not be called to endure when all the lower orders of foreigners now crowding our shores legislate for them and their daughters. Think of Patrick and Sambo and Hans and Yung Tung, who do not know the difference between a monarchy and a republic, who can not read the Declaration of Independence or Webster's spelling-book, making laws for Lucretia Mott, Ernestine L. Rose, and Anna E. Dickinson. Think of jurors and jailors drawn from these ranks to watch and try young girls for the crime of infanticide, to decide the moral code by which the mothers of this Republic shall be governed? This manhood suffrage is an appalling question, and it would be well for thinking women, who seem to consider it so magnanimous to hold

their own claims in abeyance until all men are crowned with citizenship, to remember that the most ignorant men are ever the most hostile to the equality of women, as they have known them only in slavery and degradation....

Now, when the attention of the whole world is turned to this question of suffrage, and women themselves are throwing off the lethargy of ages, and in England, France, Germany, Switzerland, and Russia are holding their conventions, and their rulers are everywhere giving them a respectful hearing, shall American statesmen, claiming to be liberal, so amend their constitutions as to make their wives and mothers the political inferiors of unlettered and unwashed ditch-diggers, boot-blacks, butchers, and barbers, fresh from the slave plantations of the South, and the effete civilizations of the Old World? While poets and philosophers, statesmen and men of science are all alike pointing to woman as the new hope for the redemption of the race, shall the freest Government on the earth be the first to establish an aristocracy based on sex alone? to exalt ignorance above education, vice above virtue, brutality and barbarism above refinement and religion? Not since God first called light out of darkness and order out of chaos, was there ever made so base a proposition as "manhood suffrage" in this American Republic, after all the discussions we have had on human rights in the last century. On all the blackest pages of history there is no record of an act like this, in any nation, where native born citizens, having the same religion, speaking the same language, equal to their rulers in wealth, family, and education, have been politically ostracised by their own countrymen, outlawed with savages, and subjected to the government of outside barbarians. Remember the Fifteenth Amendment takes in a larger population than the 2,000,000 black men on the Southern plantation. It takes in all the foreigners daily landing in our eastern cities, the Chinese crowding our western shores, the inhabitants of Alaska, and all those western isles that will soon be ours. American statesmen may flatter themselves that by superior intelligence and political sagacity the higher orders of men will always govern, but when the ignorant foreign vote already holds the balance of power in all the large cities by sheer force of numbers, it is simply a question of impulse or passion, bribery or fraud, how our elections will be carried....

Would those gentlemen who are on all sides telling the women of the nation not to press their claims until the negro is safe beyond peradventure, be willing themselves to stand aside and trust all their interests to hands like these? The educated women of this nation feel as much interest in republican institutions, the preservation of the country, the good of the race, their own elevation and success, as any man possibly can, and we have the same distrust in man's power to legislate for us, that he has in woman's power to legislate wisely for herself.

4. I would press a Sixteenth Amendment, because the history of American statesmanship does not inspire me with confidence in man's capacity to govern the nation alone, with justice and mercy. I have come to this conclusion, not only from my own observation, but from what our rulers say of themselves....

Source: Stanton, Elizabeth Cady, Susan B. Anthony, and Matilda Joslyn Gage, eds. *History of Woman Suffrage.* Vol. 2, *1861-1876.* New York: Fowler & Wells, 1882.

Divisions at the 1869 American Equal Rights Association Meeting

The following account highlights the heated disagreements that took place shortly before the women's suffrage movement divided in two rival groups. The participants in the debate are Stephen Foster, Elizabeth Cady Stanton, Mary A. Livermore, Susan B. Anthony, Henry B. Blackwell, Frederick Douglass, and Lucy Stone.

Mr. FOSTER: — …Ladies and gentlemen, I admire our talented President [Elizabeth Cady Stanton] with all my heart, and love the woman. (Great laughter.) But I believe she has publicly repudiated the principles of the society.

Mrs. STANTON:—I would like Mr. Foster to state in what way.

Mr. FOSTER: —What are these principles? The equality of men—universal suffrage. These ladies stand at the head of a paper which has adopted as its motto Educated Suffrage. I put myself on this platform as an enemy of educated suffrage, as an enemy of white suffrage, as an enemy of man suffrage, as an enemy of every kind of suffrage except universal suffrage. *The Revolution* [a newspaper that promoted women's suffrage] lately had an article headed "That Infamous Fifteenth Amendment." It is true it was not written by our President, yet it comes from a person whom she has over and over again publicly indorsed. I am not willing to take George Francis Train [a wealthy railroad financier who supported women's suffrage but made racist remarks about African Americans] on this platform with his ridicule of the negro and opposition to his enfranchisement.

Mrs. MARY A. LIVERMORE: —Is it quite generous to bring George Francis Train on this platform when he has retired from *The Revolution* entirely?

Mr. FOSTER: —If *The Revolution*, which has so often indorsed George Francis Train, will repudiate him because of his course in respect to the negro's rights, I have nothing further to say. But it does not repudiate him. He goes out; it does not cast him out.

Miss ANTHONY: —Of course it does not.

Mr. FOSTER: —My friend says yes to what I have said. I thought it was so. I only wanted to tell you why the Massachusetts society can not coalesce with the party here, and why we want these women to retire and leave us to nominate officers who can receive the respect of both parties. The Massachusetts

Abolitionists can not co-operate with this society as it is now organized. If you choose to put officers here that ridicule the negro, and pronounce the Amendment infamous, why I must retire; I can not work with you. You can not have my support, and you must not use my name. I can not shoulder the responsibility of electing officers who publicly repudiate the principles of the society.

HENRY B. BLACKWELL said: In regard to the criticisms on our officers, I will agree that many unwise things have been written in *The Revolution* by a gentleman who furnished part of the means by which that paper has been carried on. But that gentleman has withdrawn, and you, who know the real opinions of Miss Anthony and Mrs. Stanton on the question of negro suffrage, do not believe that they mean to create antagonism between the negro and the woman question. If they did disbelieve in negro suffrage, it would be no reason for excluding them. We should no more exclude a person from our platform for disbelieving negro suffrage than a person should be excluded from the anti-slavery platform for disbelieving woman suffrage. But I know that Miss Anthony and Mrs. Stanton believe in the right of the negro to vote. We are united on that point. There is no question of principle between us.

The vote on the report of the Committee on Organization was now taken, and adopted by a large majority.

Mr. DOUGLASS: —I came here more as a listener than to speak, and I have listened with a great deal of pleasure to the eloquent address of the Rev. Mr. Frothingham and the splendid address of the President. There is no name greater than that of Elizabeth Cady Stanton in the matter of woman's rights and equal rights, but my sentiments are tinged a little against *The Revolution*. There was in the address to which I allude the employment of certain names, such as "Sambo," and the gardener, and the bootblack, and the daughters of Jefferson and Washington, and all the rest that I can not coincide with. I have asked what difference there is between the daughters of Jefferson and Washington and other daughters. (Laughter.) I must say that I do not see how any one can pretend that there is the same urgency in giving the ballot to woman as to the negro. With us, the matter is a question of life and death, at least, in fifteen States of the Union. When women, because they are women, are hunted down through the cities of New York and New Orleans; when they are dragged from their houses and hung upon lamp-posts; when their children are torn from their arms, and their brains dashed out upon the pavement; when they are objects of insult and outrage at every turn; when they are in danger of having their homes burnt down over their heads; when their children are not allowed to enter schools; then they will have an urgency to obtain the ballot equal to our own. (Great applause.)

A VOICE: —Is that not all true about black women?

Mr. DOUGLASS: —Yes, yes, yes; it is true of the black woman, but not because she is a woman, but because she is black. (Applause.) Julia Ward Howe at the conclusion of her great speech delivered at the convention in Boston last year, said: "I am willing that the negro shall get the ballot before me." (Applause.) Woman! why, she has 10,000 modes of grappling with her difficulties. I believe that all the virtue of the world can take care of all the evil. I believe that all the intelligence can take care of all the ignorance. (Applause.) I am in favor of woman's suffrage in order that we shall have all the virtue and vice confronted. Let me tell you that when there were few houses in which the black man could have put his head, this woolly head of mine found a refuge in the house of Mrs. Elizabeth Cady Stanton, and if I had been blacker than sixteen midnights, without a single star, it would have been the same. (Applause.)

Miss ANTHONY: —The old anti-slavery school say women must stand back and wait until the negroes shall be recognized. But we say, if you will not give the whole loaf of suffrage to the entire people, give it to the most intelligent first. (Applause.) If intelligence, justice, and morality are to have precedence in the Government, let the question of woman be brought up first and that of the negro last. (Applause.) While I was canvassing the State with petitions and had them filled with names for our cause to the Legislature, a man dared to say to me that the freedom of women was all a theory and not a practical thing. (Applause.) When Mr. Douglass mentioned the black man first and the woman last, if he had noticed he would have seen that it was the men that clapped and not the women. There is not the woman born who desires to eat the bread of dependence, no matter whether it be from the hand of father, husband, or brother; for any one who does so eat her bread places herself in the power of the person from whom she takes it. (Applause.) Mr. Douglass talks about the wrongs of the negro; but with all the outrages that he to-day suffers, he would not exchange his sex and take the place of Elizabeth Cady Stanton. (Laughter and applause.)

Mr. DOUGLASS: —I want to know if granting you the right of suffrage will change the nature of our sexes? (Great laughter.)

Miss ANTHONY: —It will change the pecuniary position of woman; it will place her where she can earn her own bread. (Loud applause.) She will not then be driven to such employments only as man chooses for her....

Mrs. LUCY STONE: —Mrs. Stanton will, of course, advocate the precedence for her sex, and Mr. Douglass will strive for the first position for his, and both are perhaps right. If it be true that the government derives its authority from the consent of the governed, we are safe in trusting that principle to the uttermost. If one has a right to say that you can not read and therefore can not vote, then it may be said that you are a woman and therefore can not vote. We are lost if we turn away from the middle principle and argue for one class. I was once a teacher among fugitive slaves. There was one old man, and every tooth was gone, his hair was white, and his face was full of wrinkles, yet, day after day and hour after hour, he came up to the schoolhouse and tried with patience to learn to read, and by-and-by, when he had spelled out the first few verses of the first chapter of the Gospel of St. John, he said to me, "Now, I want to learn to write." I tried to make him satisfied with what he had acquired, but the old man said, "Mrs. Stone, somewhere in the wide world I have a son; I have not heard from him in twenty years; if I should hear from him, I want to write to him, so take hold of my hand and teach me." I did, but before he had proceeded in many lessons, the angels came and gathered him up and bore him to his Father. Let no man speak of an educated suffrage. The gentleman who addressed you claimed that the negroes had the first right to the suffrage, and drew a picture which only his great word-power can do. He again in Massachusetts, when it had cast a majority in favor of Grant and negro suffrage, stood upon the platform and said that woman had better wait for the negro; that is, that both could not be carried, and that the negro had better be the one. But I freely forgave him because he felt as he spoke. But woman suffrage is more imperative than his own; and I want to remind the audience that when he says what the Ku-Kluxes did all over the South, the Ku-Kluxes here in the North in the shape of men, take away the children from the mother, and separate them as completely as if done on the block of the auctioneer. Over in New Jersey they have a law which says that *any* father — he might be the most brutal man that ever existed — *any* father, it says, whether he be under age or not, may by his last will and testament dispose of the custody of his child, born or to be born, and that such disposition shall be good against all persons, and that the mother may not recover her child; and that law modified in form exists over every

State in the Union except in Kansas. Woman has an ocean of wrongs too deep for any plummet, and the negro, too, has an ocean of wrongs that can not be fathomed. There are two great oceans; in the one is the black man, and in the other is the woman. But I thank God for that XV. Amendment, and hope that it will be adopted in every State. I will be thankful in my soul if *any* body can get out of the terrible pit. But I believe that the safety of the government would be more promoted by the admission of woman as an element of restoration and harmony than the negro. I believe that the influence of woman will save the country before every other power. (Applause.) I see the signs of the times pointing to this consummation, and I believe that in some parts of the country women will vote for the President of these United States in 1872. (Applause.)

Source: Stanton, Elizabeth Cady, Susan B. Anthony, and Matilda Joslyn Gage, eds. *History of Woman Suffrage.* Vol. 2, *1861-1876.* New York: Fowler & Wells, 1882.

"The Great Secession Speech of Victoria C. Woodhull"

In the following speech, made before the National Woman's Suffrage Convention on May 11, 1871, Victoria C. Woodhull urges women to secede from the United States and form their own government if they are not granted the right to vote.

It is my conviction, arrived at after the most serious and careful consideration, that it will be equally suicidal for the Woman Suffragists to attach themselves to either [the Republican or Democratic] parties. They must not—cannot afford to—be a mere negative element in the political strife which is sure to ensue in the next Presidential election. They must assume a positive attitude upon a basis compatible with the principles of freedom, equality and justice which their enfranchisement would so gloriously demonstrate as the true principles of a republican form of government. I do not assume to speak for any one. I know I speak in direct opposition to the wishes of many by whom I am surrounded. Nevertheless, I should fail to do my duty, did I conceal what I feel to be the true interests of my sex, and through them, those of humanity; for the interests of humanity will never be understood or appreciated until women are permitted to demonstrate what they are, and how they shall be subserved. I have thus as briefly as possible given what I concieve to be the position which the Woman's Rights Party occupies at this time, their prospective power, importance and duties, and the dangers by which this country is threatened, from which they may save it.

If Congress refuse to listen to and grant what women ask, there is but one course left them to pursue. Women have no government. Men have organized a government, and they maintain it to the utter exclusion of women. Women are as much members of the nation as men are, and they have the same human right to govern themselves which men have. Men have none but an usurped right to the arbitrary control of women. Shall free, intelligent, reasoning, thinking women longer submit to being robbed of their common rights? Men fashioned a government based on their own *enunciation* of principles: that taxation without representation is tyranny; and that all just government exists by the consent of the governed. Proceeding upon *these* axioms, they formed a Constitution declaring all persons to be citizens, that one of the rights of a citizen is the right to vote, and that no power within the nation shall either make or enforce laws interfering with the citizen's rights. And yet men deny women the first and greatest of all the rights of citizenship, the right to vote.

Under such glaring inconsistencies, such unwarrantable tyranny, such unscrupulous despotism, what is there left women to do but to become the mothers of the future government.

We will have our rights. We say no longer by your leave. We have besought, argued and convinced, but we have failed; *and we will not* fail.

We will try you *just once more.* If the very next Congress refuse women all the legitimate results of citizenship; if they indeed merely so much as fail by a proper declaratory act to withdraw every obstacle to the most ample exercise of the franchise, then we give here and now, deliberate notification of what we will do next.

There is one alternative left, and we have resolved on that. This convention is for the purpose of this declaration. As surely as one year passes, from this day, and this right is not fully, frankly and unequivocally considered, we shall proceed to call another convention expressly to frame a new constitution and to erect a new government, complete in all its parts, and to take measures to maintain it as effectually as men do theirs.

If for people to govern themselves is so unimportant a matter as men now assert it to be, they could not justify themselves in interfering. If, on the contrary, it is the important thing we conceive it to be, they can but applaud us for exercising our right.

We mean treason; we mean secession, and on a thousand times grander scale than was that of the South. We are plotting revolution; we will overslough this bogus republic and plant a government of righteousness in its stead, which shall not only profess to derive its power from the consent of the governed, but shall do so in reality.

We rebel against, denounce and defy this arbitrary, usurping and tyrannical government which has been framed and imposed on us without our consent, and even without so much as entertaining the idea that it was or could be of the slightest consequence what we should think of it, or how our interests should be affected by it, or even that we existed at all, except in the simple case in which we might be found guilty of some offense against its behests, when it has not failed to visit on us its sanctions with as much rigor as if we owed rightful allegiance to it; which we do not, and which, in the future, we will not even pretend to do.

This new government, if we are compelled to form it, shall be in principles largely like that government which the better inspirations of our fathers compelled them to indite in terms in the Constitution, but from which they and their sons have so scandalously departed in their legal constructions and actual practice. It shall be applicable, not to women alone, but to all persons who shall transfer their allegance to it, and shall be in every practicable way a higher and more scientific development of the governmental idea.

We have learned the imperfections of men's government, by lessons of bitter injustice, and hope to build so well that men will desert from the less to the more perfect. And when, by our receiving justice, or by our own actions, the old and false shall be replaced by the new and true; when for tyranny and exclusiveness shall be inaugurated equality and fraternity, and the way prepared for the rapid development of social reconstruction throughout.

Because I have taken this bold and positive position; because I have advocated radical political action; because I have announced a new party and myself as a candidate for the next Presidency, I am charged with being influenced by an unwarantable ambition. Though this is scarcely the place for the introduction of a privileged question, I will, however, take this occasion to, once and for all time, state I have no personal ambition whatever. All that I have done, I did because I believed the interests of humanity would be advanced thereby.

Had I been ambitious to become the next president I should have proceeded very differently to accomplish it. I did announce myself as a candidate, and this simple fact has done a great work in compelling people to ask: and why not? This service I have rendered women at the expense of any ambition I might have had, which is apparent if the matter be but candidly considered.

In conclusion, permit me again to recur to the importance of following up the advantages we have already gained, by rapid and decisive blows for complete victory. Let us do this through the courts wherever possible, and by direct appeals to Congress during the next session. And I again declare it as my candid belief that if women will do one-half their duty until Congress meets, that they will be compelled to pass such laws as are necessary to enforce the provisions of the XIV. and XV. Articles of Amendments to the Constitution, one of which is equal political right for all citizens.

But should they fail, then for the alternative.

Source: "The Great Secession Speech of Victoria C. Woodhull before the National Woman's Suffrage Convention, at Apollo Hall, May 11, 1871." In *A History of the Woman's Rights Movement,* edited by Paulina W. Davis. 1871. Reprint, New York: Source Book Press, 1970.

Susan B. Anthony Reacts to Her Conviction for Unlawful Voting

Several women's suffrage leaders cast ballots illegally in hopes of being arrested and having their cases make their way through the courts. They believed that one case might eventually be heard by the U.S. Supreme Court, which might rule that denying women the right to vote violated the Constitution. After being convicted of unlawful voting in the November 1872 election, Susan B. Anthony made the following remarks at her sentencing.

The COURT: The prisoner will stand up. Has the prisoner anything to say why sentence shall not be pronounced?

Miss ANTHONY: Yes, your honor, I have many things to say; for in your ordered verdict of guilty, you have trampled underfoot every vital principle of our government. My natural rights, my civil rights, my political rights, are all alike ignored. Robbed of the fundamental privilege of citizenship, I am degraded from the status of a citizen to that of a subject; and not only myself individually, but all of my sex, are, by your honor's verdict, doomed to political subjection under this so-called Republican government.

Judge HUNT: The Court can not listen to a rehearsal of arguments the prisoner's counsel has already consumed three hours in presenting.

Miss ANTHONY: May it please your honor, I am not arguing the question, but simply stating the reasons why sentence can not, in justice, be pronounced against me. Your denial of my citizen's right to vote is the denial of my right of consent as one of the governed, the denial of my right of representation as one of the taxed, the denial of my right to a trial by a jury of my peers as an offender against law, therefore, the denial of my sacred rights to life, liberty, property, and—

Judge HUNT: The Court can not allow the prisoner to go on.

Miss ANTHONY: But your honor will not deny me this one and only poor privilege of protest against this high-handed outrage upon my citizen's rights. May it please the court to remember that since the day of my arrest last November, this is the first time that either myself or any person of my disfranchised class has been allowed a word of defense before judge or jury—

Judge HUNT: The prisoner must sit down; the Court can not allow it.

Miss ANTHONY: All my prosecutors, from the 8th Ward corner grocery politician, who entered the complaint, to the United States Marshal, Commissioner, District Attorney, District Judge, your honor on the bench, not one is my peer, but each and all are my political sovereigns; and had your honor submitted my case to the jury, as was clearly your duty, even then I should have had just cause of protest, for not one of those men was my peer; but, native or foreign, white or black, rich or poor, educated or ignorant, awake or asleep, sober or drunk, each and every man of them was my political superior; hence, in no sense, my peer. Even, under such circumstances, a commoner of England, tried before a jury of lords, would have far less cause to complain than should I, a woman, tried before a jury of men. Even my counsel, the Hon. Henry R. Selden, who has argued my cause so ably, so earnestly, so unanswerably before your honor, is my political sovereign. Precisely as no disfranchised person is entitled to sit upon a jury, and no woman is entitled to the franchise, so, none but a regularly admitted lawyer is allowed to practice in the courts, and no woman can gain admission to the bar—hence, jury, judge, counsel, must all be of the superior class.

Judge HUNT: The Court must insist—the prisoner has been tried according to the established forms of law.

Miss ANTHONY: Yes, your honor, but by forms of law all made by men, interpreted by men, administered by men, in favor of men, and against women; and hence, your honor's ordered verdict of guilty, against a United States citizen for the exercise of "that citizen's right to vote," simply because that citizen was a woman and not a man. But, yesterday, the same man-made forms of law declared it a crime punishable with $1,000 fine and six months' imprisonment, for you, or me, or any of us, to give a cup of cold water, a crust of bread, or a night's shelter to a panting fugitive as he was tracking his way to Canada. And every man or woman in whose veins coursed a drop of human sympathy violated that wicked law, reckless of consequences, and was justified in so doing. As then the slaves who got their freedom must take it over, or under, or through the unjust forms of law, precisely so now must women, to get their right to a voice in this Government, take it; and I have taken mine, and mean to take it at every possible opportunity.

Judge HUNT: The Court orders the prisoner to sit down. It will not allow another word.

Miss ANTHONY: When I was brought before your honor for trial, I hoped for a broad and liberal interpretation of the Constitution and its recent amendments, that should declare all United States citizens under its protecting aegis—that should declare equality of rights the national guarantee to all persons born or naturalized in the United States. But failing to get this justice—failing, even, to get a trial by a jury *not* of my peers—I ask not leniency at your hands—but rather the full rigors of the law.

Judge HUNT: The Court must insist— (Here the prisoner sat down.)

Judge HUNT: The prisoner will stand up. (Here Miss Anthony arose again.) The sentence of the Court is that you pay a fine of one hundred dollars and the costs of the prosecution.

Miss ANTHONY: May it please your honor, I shall never pay a dollar of your unjust penalty. All the stock in trade I possess is a $10,000 debt, incurred by publishing my paper—*The Revolution*—four years ago, the sole object of which was to educate all women to do precisely as I have done, rebel against your man-made, unjust, unconstitutional forms of law, that tax, fine, imprison, and hang women, while they deny them the right of representation in the Government; and I shall work on with might and main to pay every dollar of that honest debt, but not a penny shall go to this unjust claim. And I shall earnestly and persistently continue to urge all women to the practical recognition of the old revolutionary maxim, that "Resistance to tyranny is obedience to God."

Source: Stanton, Elizabeth Cady, Susan B. Anthony, and Matilda Joslyn Gage, eds. *History of Woman Suffrage*. Vol. 2, *1861-1876*. New York: Fowler & Wells, 1882.

Francis Parkman Recounts Arguments against Women's Suffrage

In the following excerpt from his booklet Some of the Reasons against Woman Suffrage, *published in 1884, Francis Parkman details some common arguments of the era against giving women the right to vote.*

THE POWER OF SEX.

Whatever liberty the best civilization may accord to women, they must always be subject to restrictions unknown to the other sex, and they can never dispense with the protecting influences which society throws about them. A man, in lonely places, has nothing to lose but life and property; and he has nerve and muscles to defend them. He is free to go whither he pleases, and run what risks he pleases. Without a radical change in human nature, of which the world has never given the faintest sign, women cannot be equally emancipated. It is not a question of custom, habit, or public opinion; but of an all-pervading force, always formidable in the vast number of men in whom it is not controlled by higher forces. A woman is subject, also, to many other restrictions, more or less stringent, necessary to the maintenance of self-respect and the respect of others, and yet placing her at a disadvantage, as compared to men, in the active work of the world. All this is mere truism, but the plainest truism may be ignored in the interest of a theory or a "cause."

Again, everybody knows that the physical and mental constitution of a woman is more delicate than in the other sex; and, we may add, the relations between mind and body are more intimate and subtle. It is true that they are abundantly so in men; but their harder organism is neither so sensitive to disturbing influences nor subject to so many of them.

It is these and other inherent conditions, joined to the engrossing nature of a woman's special functions, that have determined through all time her relative position. What we have just said — and we might have said much more — is meant as a reminder that her greatest limitations are not of human origin. Men did not make them, and they cannot unmake them. Through them, God and Nature have ordained that those subject to them shall not be forced to join in the harsh conflicts of the world militant. It is folly to ignore them, or try to counteract them by political and social quackery. They set at naught legislatures and peoples....

CRUELTY OF WOMAN SUFFRAGE.

The frequent low state of health among American women is a fact as undeniable as it is deplorable.

In this condition of things, what do certain women demand for the good of their sex? To add to the excitements that are wasting them other and greater excitements, and to cares too much for their strength other and greater cares. Because they cannot do their own work, to require them to add to it the work of men, and launch them into the turmoil where the most robust sometimes fail. It is much as if a man in a state of nervous exhaustion were told by his physician to enter at once for a foot-race or a boxing-match.

POWER SHOULD GO WITH RESPONSIBILITY.

To hold the man responsible and yet deprive him of power is neither just nor rational. The man is the natural head of the family, and is responsible for its maintenance and order. Hence he ought to control the social and business agencies which are essential to the successful discharge of the trust imposed upon him. If he is deprived of any part of this control, he should be freed also in the same measure from the responsibilities attached to it.

ALTERNATIVES OF WOMAN SUFFRAGE.

Woman suffrage must have one of two effects. If, as many of its advocates complain, women are subservient to men, and do nothing but what they desire, then woman suffrage will have no other result than to increase the power of the other sex; if, on the other hand, women vote as they see fit, without regarding their husbands, then unhappy marriages will be multiplied and divorces redoubled. We cannot afford to add to the elements of domestic unhappiness.

POLITICAL DANGERS OF WOMAN SUFFRAGE.

One of the chief dangers of popular government is that of inconsiderate and rash legislation.... This danger would be increased immeasurably if the most impulsive and excitable half of humanity had an equal voice in the making of laws, and in the administration of them....

If the better class of women flatter themselves that they can control the others, they are doomed to disappointment. They will be outvoted in their own kitchens, without reckoning the agglomerations of poverty, ignorance and vice that form a startling proportion of our city populations. It is here that the male vote alone threatens our system with its darkest perils. The female vote would enormously increase the evil, for it is often more numerous, always more impulsive and less subject to reason, and almost devoid of the sense of responsibility. Here the bad politician would find his richest resources. He could not reach the better class of female voters, but the rest would be ready to his hand....

THE FEMALE POLITICIAN.

In reckoning the resources of the female politicians, there is one which can by no means be left out. None know better than women the potency of feminine charms aided by feminine arts. The woman "inside politics" will not fail to make use of an influence so subtile and strong, and of which the management is peculiarly suited to her talents. If — and the contingency is in the highest degree probable — she is not gifted with charms of her own, she will have no difficulty in finding and using others of her sex who are. If report is to be trusted, Delilah has already spread her snares for the congressional Samson; and the power before which the wise fail and the mighty fall has been invoked against the sages and heroes of the Capitol....

MOST WOMEN AVERSE TO IT.

The agitators know well that, in spite of their persistent importunity, the majority of their sex are averse to the suffrage. Hence, the ludicrous terror which the suffragists showed at the Governor's proposal to submit the question to a vote of the women of the State....

PERMANENCE OF THE RELATIONS OF THE SEXES.

From the earliest records of mankind down to this moment, in every race and every form or degree of civilization or barbarism, the relative position of the sexes has been essentially the same, with exceptions so feeble, rare, and transient that they only prove the rule. Such permanence in the foundation of society, while all that rests upon it has passed from change to change, is proof in itself that this foundation lies deep in the essential nature of things....

The cause of this permanence is obvious. Women have great special tasks assigned them in the work of life, and men have not. To these tasks their whole nature, moral and physical, is adjusted. There is scarcely a distinctive quality of women that has not a direct or indirect bearing upon them. Everything else in their existence is subordinated to the indispensable functions of continuing and rearing the human race; and, during the best years of life, this work, fully discharged, leaves little room for any other. Rightly considered, it is a work no less dignified than essential. It is the root and stem of national existence, while the occupations of men are but the leaves and branches ....

IS WOMAN SUFFRAGE A RIGHT OR A WRONG?

It has been claimed as a right that woman should vote. It is no right, but a wrong, that a small number of women should impose on all the rest political duties which there is no call for their assuming, which they do not want to assume, and which, if duly discharged, would be a cruel and intolerable burden....

A government of glittering generalities quickly destroys itself. The object of government is the accomplishment of a certain result, the greatest good of the governed; and the ways of reaching it vary in different countries and different social conditions. Neither liberty nor the suffrage are the end; they are nothing but means to reach it; and each should be used to the extent in which it is best adapted to its purpose. If the voting of women conduces to the greatest good of the community, then they ought to vote, and otherwise they ought not. The question of female suffrage thus becomes a practical question, and not one of declamation.

WOMAN SUFFRAGE NOT PROGRESS.

Many women of sense and intelligence are influenced by the fact that the woman-suffrage movement boasts itself a movement of progress, and by a wish to be on the liberal or progressive side. But the boast is unfounded. Progress, to be genuine, must be in accord with natural law. If it is not, it ends in failure and in retrogression. To give women a thorough and wholesome training both of body and mind; to prepare such of them as have strength and opportunity for various occupations different from what they usually exercise, and above all for the practice of medicine, in which we believe that they may render valuable service; to rear them in more serious views of life and its responsibilities, are all in the way of normal and healthy development: but to plunge them into politics, where they are not needed and for which they are unfit, would be scarcely more a movement of progress than to force them to bear arms and fight ....

SHALL WE STAND BY AMERICAN PRINCIPLES?

The suffragists' idea of government is not practical, but utterly unpractical. It is not American, but French. It is that government of abstractions and generalities which found its realization in the French Revolution, and its apostle in the depraved and half-crazy man of genius, Jean Jacques Rousseau. The French had an excuse for their frenzy in the crushing oppression they had just flung off and in their inexperience of freedom. We have no excuse. Since the nation began we have been free and our liberty is in danger from nothing but its own excesses. Since France learned to subject the ideas of Rousseau to the principles of stable freedom embodied in the parliamentary government of England and in our own republicanism, she has emerged from alternate tumult and despotism to enter the paths of hope and progress....

It is not common sense alone that makes the greatness of states; neither is it sentiments and principles alone. It is these last joined with reason, reflection, and moderation. Through this union it is that one small island has become the mighty mother of nations; and it is because we ourselves, her greatest offspring, have chosen the paths of Hampden, Washington, and Franklin, and not those of Rousseau, that we have passed safe through every danger, and become the wonder and despair of despotism.

Out of the wholesome fruits of the earth, and the staff of life itself, the perverse chemistry of man distills delirious vapors, which, condensed and bottled, exalt his brain with glorious fantasies, and then leave him in the mud. So it is with the unhappy suffragists. From the sober words of our ancestors they extract the means of mental inebriety. Because the fathers of the republic gave certain reasons to emphasize their creed that America should not be taxed because America was not represented in the British Parliament, they cry out that we must fling open the floodgates to vaster tides of ignorance and folly, strengthen the evil of our system and weaken the good, feed old abuses, hatch new ones, and expose all our large cities — we speak with deliberate conviction — to the risk of anarchy.

Neither Congress, nor the States, nor the united voice of the whole people could permanently change the essential relations of the sexes. Universal female suffrage, even if decreed, would undo itself in time; but the attempt to establish it would work deplorable mischief. The question is, whether the persistency of a few agitators shall plunge us blindfold into the most reckless of all experiments; whether we shall adopt this supreme device for developing the defects of women, and demolish their real power to build an ugly mockery instead. For the sake of womanhood, let us hope not. In spite of the effect on the popular mind of the incessant repetition of a few trite fallacies, and in spite of the squeamishness that prevents the vast majority averse to the movement from uttering a word against it, let us trust that the good sense of the American people will vindicate itself against this most unnatural and pestilent revolution. In the full and normal development of womanhood lie the best interests of the world. Let us labor earnestly for it; and, that we may not labor in vain, let us save women from the barren perturbations of American politics. Let us respect them; and, that we may do so, let us pray for deliverance from female suffrage.

Source: Parkman, Francis. *Some of the Reasons against Woman Suffrage.* Printed at the Request of an Association of Women, Boston, 1884.

Belle Kearney Discusses Women's Suffrage in the South

In the southern United States, some people favored women's suffrage as a way to limit the effect of African American voting rights. In the following excerpt from a 1903 speech, Belle Kearney argues that enfranchising female voters and enacting educated suffrage requirements will help ensure "the supremacy of the white race over the African" in the South.

To day one third of the population of the South is of the negro race, and there are more negroes in the United States than there are inhabitants in "Mexico, the third Republic of the world." In some Southern States, the negroes far outnumber the whites and are so numerous in all of them as to constitute what is called a "problem." Until the present generation, they have always lived here as slaves.

The race question is national in its bearing. Still, as the South has the bulk of the negro population, the burden of the responsibility for the negro problem rests here.

The world is scarcely beginning to realize the enormity of the situation that faces the South in its grapple with the race question which was thrust upon it at the close of the Civil War, when 4,500,000 ex-slaves, illiterate and semi-barbarous, were enfranchised. Such a situation has no parallel in history. In forging a path out of the darkness, there were no precedents to lead the way. All that has been and is being accomplished is pioneer statecraft. The South has struggled under its death-weight for nearly forty years, bravely and magnanimously.

The Southern States are making a desperate effort to maintain the political supremacy of Anglo-Saxonism by amendments to their constitutions limiting the right to vote by a property and educational qualification. If the United States government had been wise enough to enact such a law when the negro was first enfranchised, it would have saved years of bloodshed in the South, and such experiences of suffering and horror among the white people here as no other were ever subjected to in an enlightened nation.

The present suffrage laws in the different Southern States can be only temporary measures for protection. Those who are wise enough to look beneath the surface will be compelled to realize the fact that they act as a stimulus to the black man to acquire both education and property, but no incentive is given to the poor whites; for it is understood, in a general way, that any man whose skin is fair enough to let the blue veins show through, may be allowed the right of franchise.

The industrial education that the negro is receiving at Tuskegee and other schools is only fitting him for power, and when the black man becomes necessary to a community by reason of his skill and acquired wealth, and the poor white man, embittered by his poverty and humiliated by his inferiority, finds no place for himself or his children, then will come the grapple between the races.

To avoid this unspeakable culmination, the enfranchisement of women will have to be effected, and an educational and property qualification for the ballot be made to apply, without discrimination, to both sexes and to both races. It will spur the poor white to keep up with the march of progression, and enable him to hold his own. The class that is not willing to measure its strength with that of an inferior is not fit to survive.

The enfranchisement of women would insure immediate and durable white supremacy, honestly attained; for, upon unquestionable authority, it is stated that "in every Southern State but one, there are more educated women than all the illiterate voters, white and black, native and foreign, combined." As you probably know, of all the women in the South who can read and write, ten out of every eleven are white. When it comes to the proportion of property between the races, that of the white outweighs that of the black immeasurably. The South is slow to grasp the fact that the enfranchisement of women would settle the race question in politics.

The civilization of the North is threatened by the influx of foreigners with their imported customs; by the greed of monopolistic wealth, and the unrest among the working classes; by the strength of the liquor traffic, and by encroachments upon religious belief.

Some day the North will be compelled to look to the South for redemption from those evils, on account of the purity of its Anglo-Saxon blood, the simplicity of its social and economic structure, the great advance in prohibitory law, and the maintenance of the sanctity of its faith, which has been kept inviolate. Just as surely as the North will be forced to turn to the South for the nation's salvation, just so surely will the South be compelled to look to its Anglo-Saxon women as the medium through which to retain the supremacy of the white race over the African.

I have heard it said in the South, "Oh, well, suffrage may be a very good thing for women in other sections of the United States, but not here. Our women are different." How are they unlike those of their own sex elsewhere? They are certainly as intelligent as any upon the face of the earth; they have the same deep love for the home, the same devotion to their country.

"Oh, yes; but, you see, if the white women were allowed to vote, the negro women would have the same privilege, and that would mean the humiliation of having to meet them at the polls on a basis of equality."

That difficulty would be settled by having separate polling places. When the ballot is given to the women of the South, you will find that these distinct voting precincts for the two races will be quickly established....

If any State, by a simple change in its election law, permits all women who can read and write and who pay a tax on property, to vote at the presidential election of 1904, the general acceptance of the women in that State would settle the question of the wisdom of woman suffrage, for the result would be vastly to increase the majority of the dominant party. Public sentiment would undergo such a revolution as to make a subsequent amendment to the State constitution, bestowing unlimited enfranchisement upon women, easy to obtain.

The South, which has wrought so splendidly in the past, surely will measure up to its responsibility in taking the forward step of woman's enfranchisement in order to render justice to its own firesides and to fix the status of the white race for future years.

Anglo Saxonism is the standard of the ages to come. It is, above all else, the granite foundation of the South. Upon that its civilization will mount; upon that it will stand unshaken.

The white people of the North and South are children of the same heroic souls who laid the foundations of civil and religious liberty in this new world, and built thereon this great Republic. We call to you, men and women, across that invisible line that divides the sections, across the passage of deathless years, to unite with us in holding this mighty country safe for the habitation of the Anglo-Saxon.

Thank God the black man was freed! I wish for him all possible happiness and all possible progress, but not in encroachments upon the holy of holies of the Anglo-Saxon race.

Source: Kearney, Belle. "The South and Woman Suffrage." *Woman's Journal* 34, no. 14 (4 April 1903): 106-107.

Picketing and Prison: The Experiences of Ernestine Hara Kettler

The radical National Woman's Party began sending groups of female protesters to picket in front of the White House in January 1917. They planned to oppose President Woodrow Wilson until he agreed to support a constitutional amendment granting women the right to vote. As the pickets stretched on for months, hundreds of women were arrested and sent to prison. In the following account, protester Ernestine Hara Kettler recalls her experiences on the picket line and in prison.

I met Katherine Hodges.... We started talking and she told me about the National Woman's Party in Washington, D.C., whose members were picketing the president. She asked if I cared to go. Of course, anything as exciting as that would have appealed to me.

I might have been taken as an adventurer because during that time I was having a good time. I had walked in the suffrage parade of 1915, or whenever it was, but I wasn't fighting for feminism. I was interested in the theater, in writing, in art. I was a bohemian in the real sense of the word....

I don't know how this conversation with Katherine Hodges started, but she told me what the suffrage party was doing in Washington—the picket lines and so on—and said that I might be sent to jail. Well, I'd never been to jail. It was kind of romantic in my mind. I thought it would be a thrilling experience. I was both serious and light-headed about it. Not light-hearted, but just a little light-headed....

But it wasn't just an adventure. As a radical, I believed in justice. It was very just for women to vote and it was highly undemocratic and an outrage that so much opposition had been placed against their getting the ballot. There were, after all, as many women in the country as men. What is this business? Is a woman so far below a man intellectually that she's not fit to vote? When I think of it, it's just incredible! I can't believe it! I was actually outraged that women didn't have the vote! That's why I went down to Washington, D.C.

I don't know how I got there. I didn't have money, so someone must have paid my fare down there, perhaps this Katherine Hodges or the suffrage party. All I remember is I found myself in Washington, and that I was met at the station and taken to the headquarters of the National Woman's Party. The headquarters was the Little White House; that's where President McKinley died. I was given his room and his bed. I wanted to get out of that room, fast. I didn't want to sleep in anybody's deathbed. Of course he was only killed, you know, he didn't die of a disease.

What they were doing was picketing in groups of four. Each group had a shift. As soon as one group was arrested, then they sent out another group of four. There was a continuous picket line. That's what drove the policemen crazy—they saw no end to the number of women who were picketing!

I met the other three women in my group at the headquarters. One of them was Peggy Johns from New York. Another, whose name I do not remember, was an organizer in the needle trades in New York. The fourth was a lawyer from one of the Western states, either Wyoming or Arizona. They were all between twenty-five and thirty-five. I was the youngest in the group, twenty-one.

We started picketing the second or third day I was there. We walked back and forth, right in front of the White House gates. We had a banner, but I don't remember whether we each carried one banner or whether the four of us carried one long one with four posts on it. There must have been a saying on it. You can't just have a plain banner without something on it to draw the attention of the people passing by.

A pretty big crowd would gather every day—at least it seemed pretty big to me. There were always men and women standing there harassing us and throwing some pretty bad insults—and pretty obscene ones. The women weren't obscene, but the men were. Our instructions were to pay absolutely no attention to them. I ignored them. I was brave. My goodness, I was fighting for a cause.

We had some support, but they took their lives in their hands. If any of the bystanders supported us, they could be beaten by the rest of the crowd. Towards the end, they started throwing stuff at the women. In fact, during this period somebody fired a shot through the windows of the Little White House, the headquarters. Any woman who happened to be in the right position for it could have been killed. And we couldn't get police protection. We just couldn't get it. The only protection we had was when we were arrested. Then we were protected!...

On one of the picketing days, the police hauled us in and took us to jail. All four of us. Immediately the lawyer or somebody was sent to the city jail to bail us out, so we were in jail only about an hour or so. We didn't have to wait too many days for our trial. After all, the National Woman's Party had to board us, and that costs money.

At the trial we all made statements that we were not obstructing traffic, but that traffic was obstructing us—which was true. Obstructing traffic and loitering were the charges. We weren't doing either one of them. We were marching. "There were only four of us," we told them, "so we couldn't possibly obstruct traffic. We were on the sidewalk, there was only one row of us, only four of us. There was plenty of room. But unfortunately a lot of people stopped and they obstructed traffic. None of them were arrested, except us." We were very bold.

The judge asked how old I was, and when I said twenty-one, he was so mad. He scowled. He couldn't believe it because he knew that the suffrage party was insistent about that; we had to be twenty-one or over, otherwise we couldn't march.

So we were given thirty days. Before then, only the hard-core criminals like Alice Paul had been given thirty days. After we were sentenced, we were taken to the city jail. That's where we cooked up our political prisoner demands: We were political prisoners. We were not guilty of obstructing traffic. We were not guilty of the sentence as charged. Therefore, we did not owe any kind of work in the workhouse. That workhouse in Occoquan, Virginia, was a real workhouse—you worked or else.

We made all these decisions in the city jail where we were taken and kept overnight. That really gave quite a different tinge to the whole struggle. Peggy Johns was the one who suggested it. She was the truly political person in that group. We all agreed with her. I'm surprised that the trade unionist didn't mention it first, but a trade unionist doesn't necessarily find her experience in political prisoner activities. I didn't even think of it.

The next morning we were taken in a bus to Occoquan Workhouse [also spelled Occuquan]. When we got there we had an immediate discussion with the other women and told them our decision. There was already a group of either eight or twelve of our women there. They were very enthusiastic about the idea and accepted it, without question. The next day we appeared in the workroom and we just sat there with our hands in our laps.

All the women in that sewing room took an example from us. I think there were probably about a dozen other women in that room. When they saw we weren't working, they took heart. They could be real courageous. They wouldn't work either. There was nothing that could be done about the whole room. I think that's what bothered the superintendent. He wouldn't have cared so much if the others had continued to work.

It wasn't long before he asked if we would at least, please, hold the work in our laps. We were demoralizing the other prisoners in that workroom. I suppose we were to be making sack dresses; that's all we wore, just sack dresses. We said, "No. We decided that since we were unjustly arrested and that we were political prisoners, it would be just as wrong for us to hold the work in our hands as it would be to sew it. We were going to abide by our decision—that we had to be respected as political prisoners."

We'd go to the workroom and we'd just sit there all day long. We talked, you know. All we could do was talk. Since we were all sitting at one table, we did a great deal of talking as to how to comport ourselves. We lived in dormitories; we slept in one long dormitory with beds on both sides, about three feet apart from each other. It was just like the ones you see in motion pictures of prison wards or hospitals. There were about thirty in the dormitory—not just suffragists, but other prisoners, too. We took turns washing ourselves every morning. There were several sinks and we took turns. Then we went into the dining room.

I think twice a day we went out for our "constitutional." We had certain prescribed prison walks through the gardens there; it was a lovely fall time of the year, you know. The leaves were turning red and they were falling, the air was fresh.

We were allowed some correspondence, but that was limited to receiving books, letters and newspapers from our relatives and friends. To my knowledge, I was the only one who was permitted a visit; my mother was permitted to come and see me. The people in the office were mad as hell because we spoke in Rumanian and nobody understood.

The food was the greatest problem we had there. It was just unbelievable—the worms that were found in the oatmeal we ate, in the soup we ate. I don't remember anything else. The coffee was God knows what—it wasn't coffee. It might have been chicory. To me that was the most terrible part of the whole prison experience, the food.

We all suffered. This was before the hunger strike, but some of the women were actually on a hunger strike already! They just couldn't eat. The only thing they could eat was bread, if it wasn't totally moldy and if it didn't show rat tracks. That prison was paid hundreds of thousands of dollars to feed us, and it raised beautiful vegetables, but we had none of them. Instead, they bought this old stuff that was rancid and sitting in warehouses heaven knows how many years, and fed us that.

In those days a lot of food had worms in it; you had to be careful. When you bought it, you had to eat it right away. The prison didn't buy the food right away or didn't cook it right away, and it bought the worst of all possible foods, anyway. It was all loaded with worms. I just didn't know what to do; I used to pick out the worms. If I found some clean oatmeal or clean soup, I'd eat it. But most of us lost a lot of pounds during the thirty days in that work-house. I just couldn't go through the job of picking out the worms, weevils, or whatever they were. It was really miserable in that fashion. Otherwise we weren't punished. There was nothing the superintendent could do if you refused to work. There was only one occasion when we actually suffered brutality. You see, my friend Peggy Johns became ill and was taken to the hospital. I used to visit her in the hospital every day. One day I went to see her and she wasn't there. I asked the nurse what happened and she said she didn't know. I asked all the other nurses, whoever was there, and they all said, "We don't know. Just go ask the superintendent."

I rushed into the other building. There was a long hall with a dining room at one end and the superintendent's office at the other. As I walked along the hallway, there was Peggy—all dressed up in her civilian clothes. "Peggy," I said, "where are you going?" "They're taking me to the psychopathic ward in Washington, D.C. Go tell the other girls, and all of you rush back here." So I did.

We all rushed back to the superintendent's office. He was absolutely dumbfounded when he saw us. He thought he'd be able to steal her away without us knowing. If I hadn't been such a loyal visitor, we wouldn't have found out. When we got into that office, we told him he couldn't do that, that she would have to be picked up by our lawyer in Washington and taken to the hospital, and that she couldn't be sent just by the prison alone, that we had no assurance what would happen to her, and that, above all things, we wanted security for our women.

He wouldn't abide by it. One of the women rushed to the telephone to phone our headquarters in Washington, and he rushed over, too, and just tore the phone right off the wall. Then he called in deputies. Of all the dirty tricks, he called in Negro girls to come in there, and I'm telling you, they beat the hell out of us. I was so little that I was scared to death to get in the crowd and I was on the outside.

I saw women on the floor, being trampled. The Negro girls—considering how badly they were treated—got the most intense joy out of beating the hell out of the white women. The superintendent was frightened when he saw the zeal with which these women were beating us. He didn't want us killed or hurt in any way because he would be held entirely responsible, so he had to call in the men deputies to haul the Negro girls off us and get them outside. He then allowed us to call Washington, and we told them at headquarters what was going on. So Peggy was sent to Washington, and the lawyer met her and took her to the hospital, or wherever it was. Anyway, it wasn't the psychopathic ward....

The next day, after this fracas, they sent us back to the city jail. The superintendent didn't want us there any longer at the workhouse and he maneuvered to send us to the city jail to finish out our sentence. We had about three days left to serve. We had lost our automatic five days off for good behavior after the first day we were in city jail. Or perhaps we had lost it at the workhouse because we initiated that work strike.

In the city jail we raised Cain! I remember that after we ate, we'd take the tin plates and throw them through the bars of the gate, of the doors, right at the windows. I think we broke some windows. We raised so much hell. We had all kinds of notoriety. The newspapermen came to interview us. They'd even bring us food from the outside. The food in the city jail was much better than at the workhouse. But we were mad; we were so darned mad. They put us in solitary confinement, two in each cell. We were held there in the city jail three days and then released.

The next group that came in was the one that went on a hunger strike, and they were brutally treated. They received very severe treatment. They were beaten and dragged across the patio from the superintendent's office to their cells. (These later women were segregated; they were put in cells.) Some women had broken ribs and were bleeding profusely and they weren't treated. Others had all kinds of lacerations.

After we were released from jail we went back to headquarters. I don't know how long I stayed there, perhaps another week or two. I was even tempted to go back again on the picket line, but I just couldn't stand the thought of going back to that workhouse again. After thirty days of that dreadful food and the fear of what might happen to the next contingent that was arrested, I just wasn't courageous enough to go back again. I felt horrified by the different things that could happen to you in prison. It wasn't as exciting as I had thought it would be; it was exciting in a frightening way, but not exciting in a joyous way. That was one reason I decided not to go back again on the picket line and then be tried again and sentenced again....

I don't think any of the women in my contingent signed for another commitment. The only one I kept in touch with was Peggy Johns. She wasn't much taller than I am. Maybe we just stood together and supported one another; it gave us this additional muscle that we needed. There didn't seem to be any bond with the others and I never saw any of them again except for Peggy. She was in New York, too, and until I went West I saw quite a bit of her....

I don't recall any of the other women that I met in Washington, except Alice Paul. My impression of her was of a very serious and dedicated woman. Most of the women were liberal-conservative. They were not radicals; their vision was limited to voting rights.... Many of them came from fine, rich families with very good minds and a willingness to fight for their ideas; to endure prison and the food and to even starve if they couldn't eat the food. One woman was terribly sick when she was taken out of there. She came from a wealthy family, and going to prison was a real sacrifice for her. Two of those women had husbands or fathers who were senators or representatives in Congress.

I sure felt awfully sorry for those women. After all, I came from a poor family. They weren't poor like I was, and they could be very choosy about their food, and very demanding. But this was the first time I confronted worms, and these were outstanding because there were so many of them. You know, for about thirty years afterwards, I couldn't eat oatmeal or soup in a restaurant. It just sickened me, just the mere thought of it. And to this day, I keep searching for things in it. This is the lasting effect jail had on me.

Source: "Ernestine Hara Kettler: In Prison." In *From Parlor to Prison: Five American Suffragists Talk about Their Lives*, edited by Sherna Gluck. New York: Vintage Books, 1976.

The Nineteenth Amendment

The following amendment giving women the right to vote became part of the United States Constitution on August 26, 1920.

Section 1. The right of citizens of the United States to vote shall not be denied or abridged by the United States or by any State on account of sex.

Section 2. Congress shall have power to enforce this article by appropriate legislation.

SOURCES FOR FURTHER STUDY

Books

Buhle, Mari Jo, and Paul Buhle. *The Concise History of Woman Suffrage: Selections from the Classic Work of Stanton, Anthony, Gage, and Harper.* Urbana, IL: University of Illinois Press, 1978. A shortened and annotated version of the classic multi-volume historical study *History of Woman Suffrage,* which was put together by several of the legendary women's-rights pioneers.

Goldsmith, Barbara. *Other Powers: The Age of Suffrage, Spiritualism, and the Scandalous Victoria Woodhull.* New York: Knopf, 1998. Fascinating account of Woodhull's life that also discusses other prominent figures in the nineteenth-century suffrage movement and the historical and social factors that shaped them.

Gurko, Miriam. *The Ladies of Seneca Falls: The Birth of the Woman's Rights Movement.* New York: Macmillan, 1974. An interesting, easy-to-read chronicle of the early leaders of the women's suffrage movement.

Ward, Geoffrey C. *Not For Ourselves Alone: The Story of Elizabeth Cady Stanton and Susan B. Anthony.* New York: Knopf, 1999. A photo-rich biography of Stanton and Anthony that serves as the book version of the documentary film of the same name (see below).

Video

Iron Jawed Angels (DVD). HBO Video. 2004. A dramatized but fairly accurate depiction of the National Woman's Party's crusade in the 1910s, focusing on the relationship between Alice Paul and Lucy Burns.

Not for Ourselves Alone: The Story of Elizabeth Cady Stanton and Susan B. Anthony (VHS). PBS Home Video. 1999. A lengthy documentary by Ken Burns and Paul Barnes that traces the lives of these famed suffragists and their influence on the nineteenth-century suffrage movement.

BIBLIOGRAPHY

Books and Periodicals

Adams, Mildred. *The Right to Be People.* Philadelphia, PA: J. B. Lippincott, 1967.

Benjamin, Anne M. *A History of the Anti-Suffrage Movement in the United States from 1895 to 1920: Women against Equality.* Lewiston, NY: Edwin Mellen Press, 1991.

Buhle, Mari Jo, and Paul Buhle. *The Concise History of Woman Suffrage: Selections from the Classic Work of Stanton, Anthony, Gage, and Harper.* Urbana, IL: University of Illinois Press, 1978.

Camhi, Jane Jerome. *Women against Women: American Anti-Suffragism, 1880-1920.* Brooklyn, NY: Carlson, 1994.

Clift, Eleanor. *Founding Sisters and the Nineteenth Amendment.* Hoboken, NJ: John Wiley & Sons, 2003.

Ford, Linda G. *Iron-Jawed Angels: The Suffrage Militancy of the National Woman's Party, 1912-1920.* Lanham, MD: University Press of America, 1991.

Gluck, Sherna, ed. *From Parlor to Prison: Five American Suffragists Talk about Their Lives.* New York: Vintage, 1976.

Goldsmith, Barbara. *Other Powers: The Age of Suffrage, Spiritualism, and the Scandalous Victoria Woodhull.* New York: Knopf, 1998.

Graham, Sara Hunter. *Woman Suffrage and the New Democracy.* New Haven, CT: Yale University Press, 1996.

Gurko, Miriam. *The Ladies of Seneca Falls: The Birth of the Woman's Rights Movement.* New York: Macmillan, 1974.

Hahn, Emily. *Once upon a Pedestal.* New York: Thomas Y. Crowell, 1974.

Harvey, Anna L. *Votes without Leverage: Women in American Electoral Politics: 1920-1970.* Cambridge, UK: Cambridge University Press, 1998.

Howard, Angela M., and Frances M. Kavenik. *Handbook of American Women's History.* 2d edition. Thousand Oaks, CA: Sage, 2000.

Irwin, Inez Hayes. *The Story of Alice Paul and the National Woman's Party.* Fairfax, VA: Denlinger's Publishers, 1977.

Keyssar, Alexander. *The Right to Vote: The Contested History of Democracy in the United States.* New York: Basic Books, 2000.

Kleppner, Paul. "Were Women to Blame? Female Suffrage and Voter Turnout." *Journal of Interdisciplinary History* 12, Spring 1982.

Klosko, George, and Margaret G. Klosko. *The Struggle for Women's Rights: Theoretical and Historical Sources.* Upper Saddle River, NJ: Prentice-Hall, 1999.

Kornbluh, Mark Lawrence. *Why America Stopped Voting: The Decline of Participatory Democracy and the Emergence of Modern American Politics.* New York: New York University Press, 2000.

Kraditor, Aileen S. *The Ideas of the Woman Suffrage Movement, 1890-1920.* New York: Norton, 1981.

Kugler, Israel. *From Ladies to Women: The Organized Struggle for Women's Rights in the Reconstruction Era.* New York: Greenwood, 1987.

Lunardini, Christine A. *From Equal Suffrage to Equal Rights: Alice Paul and the National Woman's Party, 1910-1928.* New York: New York University Press, 1986.

Marilley, Suzanne M. *Woman Suffrage and the Origins of Liberal Feminism in the United States.* Cambridge, MA: Harvard University Press, 1996.

Mead, Rebecca J. *How the Vote was Won: Woman Suffrage in the Western United States, 1868-1914.* New York: New York University Press, 2004.

Merriman, Charles E., and Harold F. Gosnell. *Nonvoting: Causes and Methods of Control.* Chicago: University of Chicago Press, 1924.

Scott, Anne F., and Andrew M. Scott. *One Half the People: The Fight for Woman Suffrage.* Philadelphia: J. B. Lippincott, 1975.

Stanton, Elizabeth Cady, Susan B. Anthony, and Matilda Joslyn Gage, eds. *History of Woman Suffrage.* Vol. 1, *1848-1861.* New York: Fowler & Wells, 1881.

———. *History of Woman Suffrage.* Vol. 2, *1861-1876.* New York: Fowler & Wells, 1882.

———. *History of Woman Suffrage.* Vol. 3. *1876-1885.* Rochester, NY: Charles Mann, 1887.

Stevens, Doris. *Jailed for Freedom.* New York: Boni and Liveright, 1920.

Terborg-Penn, Rosalyn. *African American Women in the Struggle for the Vote, 1850-1920.* Bloomington, IN: Indiana University Press, 1998.

Tompkins, Vincent, ed. *American Decades: 1910-1919.* Detroit, MI: Gale Research, 1996.

Ward, Geoffrey C. *Not For Ourselves Alone: The Story of Elizabeth Cady Stanton and Susan B. Anthony.* New York: Knopf, 1999.

Weatherford, Doris. *A History of the American Suffragist Movement.* Santa Barbara, CA: ABC-CLIO, 1998.

Wheeler, Marjorie Spruill, ed. *One Woman, One Vote: Rediscovering the Woman Suffrage Movement.* Troutdale, OR: New Sage Press, 1995.

———. *Votes for Women! The Woman Suffrage Movement in Tennessee, the South, and the Nation.* Knoxville, TN: University of Tennessee Press, 1995.

Online

American President.org. "William Howard Taft" (citing voter participation in presidential elections 1840-1900). http://www.americanpresident.org/history/h_home.shtml

"The Equal Rights Amendment." http://www.equalrightsamendment.org/

Center for American Women and Politics. "Women in Elected Office 2005." http://www.cawp.rutgers.edu/Facts/Officeholders/cawpfs.html

Fairvote. "Presidential Election Voter Turnout, 1924-2000." http://www.fairvote.org/turnout/preturn.htm

Harvard University Library Open Collections Program: Women Working, 1870-1930. "General Federation of Women's Clubs." http://ocp.hul.harvard.edu/ww/organizations-federation.html

The Triangle Factory Fire. http://www.ilr.cornell.edu/trianglefire/

U.S. Census Bureau. "National Population Estimates – Characteristics." http://www.census.gov/popest/national/asrh/NC-EST2003-as.html

U.S. Census Bureau. "Voting and Registration in the Election of November 2000." http://www.census.gov/prod/2002pubs/p20-542.pdf

Women in American History by Encyclopedia Britannica. "Woman's Journal." http://search.eb.com/women/articles/Woman's_Journal.html

Women in History. "Alice Paul." http://www.lkwdpl.org/wihohio/paul-ali.htm

Infoplease. "The Wage Gap: A History of Pay Inequity and the Equal Pay Act." http://www.infoplease.com/spot/equalpayact1.html

Video

Iron Jawed Angels (DVD). HBO Video. 2004.

Not for Ourselves Alone: The Story of Elizabeth Cady Stanton and Susan B. Anthony (VHS). PBS Home Video. 1999.

PHOTO CREDITS

INDEX

(ill.) denotes illustration